The A–Z of Microlighting

The A–Z of Microlighting

CHRIS STOW

THE CROWOOD PRESS

First published in 2006 by
The Crowood Press Ltd
Ramsbury, Marlborough
Wiltshire SN8 2HR

www.crowood.com

British Library Cataloguing-in-Publication Data
A catalogue record for this book is available from the British Library.

ISBN 1 86126 808 4
EAN 978 1 86126 808 2

Frontispiece courtesy of P&M Aviation.

Typefaces used: Galliard and Helvetica.

Typeset and designed by
D & N Publishing
Lambourn Woodlands, Hungerford, Berkshire.

Printed and bound in Singapore by Craft Print International.

CONTENTS

Preface

Microlights have been flying in the UK in their present form since about the early 1980s, and many good books have been written on the topic. This manual is a quick reference to everyday information that a new student or an existing pilot will require.

The author started his aviation career some twenty years ago, flying with a friend in a Beagle Pup. He got the 'bug' and started having lessons, but a badly organized school with part-time instructors and not many lessons didn't help him realize his dream. His training discontinued, money and work forced him to put the idea on the back burner. A former girlfriend sparked the light again by buying him a trial lesson in a Cessna aircraft, and this time more money, availability of instructors and a well-organized school meant that the process of learning to fly became a reality.

His licence gained, he wanted more, and he knew he was destined to become an instructor. As the cost of obtaining a commercial licence was prohibitive, he decided to add a microlight rating to his licence; so he started on the route to becoming a microlight instructor.

Now a fully qualified instructor with many instructional hours under his belt – on both weight-shift and 3-axis types – he has ample time, when the British weather forces him and his students to remain on the ground, to write manuals and prepare literature, for the good of the sport.

This book is really a glossary of terms, wittily written, but still explaining the realities of microlighting in a serious way. I have included the microlight syllabus for both 3-axis and weight-shift aircraft because it is my belief that the ground subjects and the flying go hand in hand.

Enjoy the read, enjoy the fun, and long may you continue to live your dreams in the sky. For those of you who wish to become pilots: do it, do it now – I guarantee you will never have a dull moment.

Happy and safe flying.

CHRIS STOW

The A–Z of Microlighting

THE AIRCRAFT RADIO LICENCE

An aircraft radio licence is required for all radio equipment fitted to an aircraft. The CAA issue licences for fixed installations and also the 'Aircraft Transportable Licence', for a handheld that can be used in any aircraft. The price is the same for either.

To operate a radio in the air, you must be in possession of a 'Flight Radio Telephony Operators Licence' (FRTOL). The wavebands in the UK are crowded with people who cannot use a radio: it can be quite comical listening to a stuttering pilot getting his/her knickers in a twist. This can also be true, however, of pilots who possess the licence – remember that the radio is not a CB with which to talk to your mates over the airwaves.

AIRSPACE CLASSES

The airspace of the United Kingdom is divided into the following classes:

Class A airspace All airways, and certain defined Control Zones (CTRs), Control Terminal Areas (CTAs) and Terminal Manoeuvring Areas (TMAs).

Class B airspace Upper airspace (above FL 245).

Class C airspace None allocated at present.

Class D airspace Defined CTRs and CTAs.

Class E airspace As and when defined. At present: the Scottish TMA, at and below 6,000ft AMSL, the Belfast TMA, and the Scottish CTR outside Glasgow and Prestwick CTRs.

Class F airspace Advisory routes.

Class G airspace Open airspace.

AXIS

In the microlight world we have two distinct forms of aircraft: 2-axis, generally known as weight-shift or flex-wing aircraft; and 3-axis, or fixed-wing aircraft. The weight-shift aircraft are the ones that the general public associate with microlights. When people discover what I do for a living they generally say 'Oh you fly one of those hang-gliders with an engine on the back.' Of course I put them straight with their description, but technically they are correct.

The weight-shift microlight was developed when some hang-glider pilots became tired of waiting for the right weather to get aloft, so they developed 'trike' units fitted with seats and engines to help them do so.

On weight-shift aircraft there are two axes of movement, longitudinal and lateral, or 'roll' and 'pitch'. Roll is the method by which weight-shift aircraft turn in the air, and pitch is the method by which we speed up or slow down the aircraft.

Pitch is longitudinal movement around the lateral axis. If you change the angle of attack, by moving the leading edge of the wing in relation to the airflow, it alters the amount of

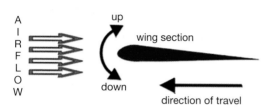

Airflow wing section.

drag the wing creates: leading edge down = less drag and more airspeed; leading edge up = more drag and less airspeed.

Roll control is achieved by altering the angle at which each wing meets the airflow, so that as roll control is input one wing speeds up and the other slows down, thus enabling a turn to be completed. *See also* 'Billow Shift'.

On 3-axis aircraft the same principles apply, except that the controls move surfaces on the wing and the tailplane, altering the movement of airflow over these surfaces. The elevators control pitch, the ailerons control roll and the rudder controls yaw.

While weight-shift aircraft are inherently stable in roll and pitch, they aren't directionally stable. The 3-axis types, with a rudder for yaw control, are directionally stable.

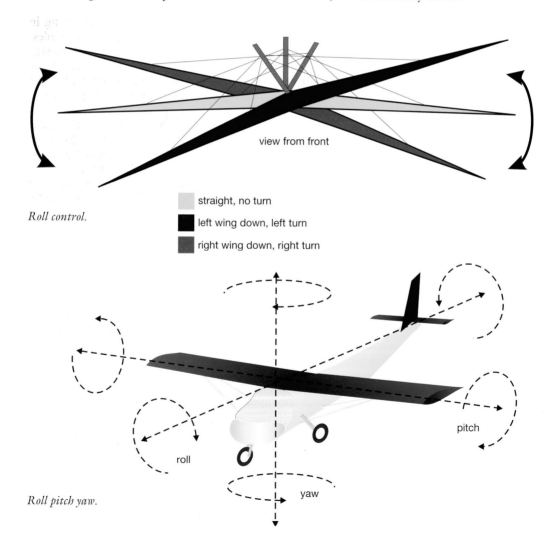

Roll control.

Roll pitch yaw.

THE BASIC EXERCISES

These include: taxying – how we taxi the aircraft safely and efficiently; straight and level flight, which deals with flying the aircraft in a straight line, at a constant altitude, and at differing airspeeds; climbing and descending; and medium-level turns, up to 30 degrees. During Exercises 1 and 2 you will be familiarized with the aircraft and shown how to prepare it for flight; Exercise 3 is a straightforward 'air experience' flight.

Exercise 4 – The Effects of Controls Exercise 4 is possibly the first time you will actually fly the aircraft, and feel what each control does. You will soon realize that each control input has both a primary and a secondary effect, and of course the right effect, the movement we want to achieve.

Exercise 5 – Taxiying This is a big deal, especially in a weight-shift aircraft as these are more susceptible to accidents on the ground than in the air. You will be taught how to taxi safely and efficiently, by use of all the controls, to keep all your wheels on terra firma until you need to be airborne.

Exercise 6 – Straight and Level Flight This can be difficult for an early student to grasp, as it involves keeping an accurate heading at the same time as an accurate altitude, and then doing the same at faster and slower airspeeds.

Exercises 7 and 8 – Climbing and Descending This is down to coordination of all the controls, using mnemonics such as PAT, PAHT, AHPT and APT, where P = power, A = attitude, H = hold and T = trim.

Exercises 9a and 9b – Medium-Level Turns Turns up to and including 30 degrees of bank, these again mean using coordination skills to maintain a constant altitude during the turn. Coordination skills also apply in climbing and descending turns.

BATTENS

These keep the upper surface of the wing in the shape it was intended, and in their simplest form are simply wing stiffeners. Nearly all rag-and-tube microlights have wing battens. They vary in length on weight-shift types, the longest being at the root of the wing and the shortest at the tips. 3-axis types have them, too.

Battens can become mis-shaped, which can cause handling problems. This is usually nothing really serious – a turn to the left or right can be the result of a mis-shaped batten. Usually an experienced pilot or aircraft inspector can 'tweak' the battens to make the aircraft fly hands-off in perfect trim.

BILLOW-SHIFT

This is an aid to turning in a weight-shift aircraft. If you sit in a weight-shift aircraft and look up at the point where wing meets trike, there is an inspection hole in the underside of

Billow-shift.

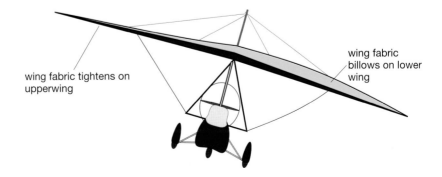

wing fabric tightens on upperwing

wing fabric billows on lower wing

the fabric. While looking into this hole, move the wing in a roll-right to roll-left movement: it should be evident that the whole wing moves independently to the keel tube. This 'floating cross tube' has a good effect in the air: the fabric, during a turn while in flight, will shift and billow. This billow-shift changes the angle of attack of the upper and lower wings: the upper wing tries to move faster than the lower one, creating a turn.

THE BMAA

The British Microlight Aircraft Association (BMAA) is a Civil Aviation Authority-approved organization that has powers to control training and airworthiness in microlights. It looks after the interests of its members by aiming to further the sport of microlighting, by representing its members in national and international matters.

The association has several full-time helpful and knowledgeable staff, who are always willing to pass on supportive information. Headed by the Chief Executive, there is technical staff, an office staff and a council (which is voluntary).

The BMAA organizes an annual show and AGM for its members to attend, and produces a magazine that is only available to members. The BMAA website is www.bmaa.org.

CHECKS

Aviation in any form is a potentially dangerous activity and checks are performed to minimize the risk of accident and injury. There are many checks, but they are all there for a reason.

Most aircraft have their own set of checks. The main check that any pilot must make is the daily inspection of the aircraft, a thorough and full check of every conceivable item on the aircraft, every moving part, every control, every surface of the wings and fuselage, and so on. Checks are usually mnemonics to make them easy to remember. The following are fairly generic and can be used for most aircraft types:

Pre-Start Check

S Security: seat belts fastened and secure, helmets fastened, brakes on
T Throttles off, choke on if required
A Area check: check for other aircraft, people and so on
M Masters and magnetos on
P Prop: shout 'Clear Prop' in a loud voice, one last look around and start

Once the aircraft has started, move to a safe area to carry on with the next check.

Pre-Take-Off Check

This check tells the pilot that the controls, engine and instruments are working, and that his passenger is secure. It is also the last chance before flight to check that the fuel is on and there is sufficient for flight. The pre-take-off check, or 'vital actions':

C Controls moving fully and freely, and working correctly
H Harnesses and helmets secure
I Instruments working and set as required
E Engine up to temperature, pressures all in the green, magneto drop check
F Fuel sufficient for flight

T Trim set as required (3-axis), tangs and pins check (weight-shift)

A Area in the circuit and ground clear for manoeuvring, wind check

P Power: full power check (usually performed on the take-off run)

En-Route Check

L Location, be aware of where you are, airspace restrictions, and so on

I Indications, temperatures and pressures all okay

F Fuel: enough for remainder of journey

T Time elapsed: how much endurance do you have left?

I use this check every 15–20 minutes.

Shut-Down Check

Should an emergency happen in the air, a check is needed to close down the aircraft in sequence:

T Throttles off (in case the engine should start again)

I Ignitions and master off (master off only after a radio call has been made)

F Fuel tap off

S Security: pilot and passenger secure, hatches unlatched, brief passenger if time permits

Join/Rejoin Check

After a flight has been completed then a rejoin or joining Check is required:

R Radio call made to obtain information regarding runway in use and QFE

A Airfield and area checked for other traffic and the airfield is usable

F Fuel enough for a go-around if needed

T Throttle/Trim: hand throttles off (weight-shift), trim set (3-axis)

Downwind Check

When an aircraft has rejoined the circuit a downwind check should be performed. For weight-shift aircraft I use:

F Fuel enough for a go-around

A Area: be aware of other traffic

W Wind correct for runway in use

N Nosewheel straight, brakes off

T Throttle: hand throttle off

S Security: seatbelts secure, both pilot and passenger

For 3-axis I use:

T Trim set

W Wind correct for runway

A Area: aware of other traffic

S Security: seatbelts, hatches and so on

F Fuel sufficient for go-around

U Undercarriage – a wheel either side would be good!

N Needles, temperatures and pressures all okay

Pre-Stall Check

During training a student is taught a pre-stall check, which is only really to make sure that enough leeway is there for recovery should anything go wrong. If the aircraft stalls during normal flight this check cannot be performed, so it is only relevant to practising stall recovery.

H Height: sufficient to recover by 1,000ft AGL

A Airframe suitable for the manoeuvre

S Security: no loose objects and seatbelts are secure

E Engine temperatures and pressures all okay

L Location: not over a built up area, etc

L Lookout: a good lookout above, below and all round

Pilot Check

One final check: is the pilot okay to fly:

I Illness: is the pilot well?

M Medicines: is the pilot taking any drugs that could impede his or her ability?

S Stress: is the pilot under any stress?

A Alcohol: eight hours bottle to throttle?

F Fatigue: is the pilot well rested?

E Eaten: has the pilot eaten?

CLOUDS

Clouds come in many differing forms and varieties. What follows are some photographs taken by the author, so you know what you are looking at:

COMPASS

An instrument that always points to magnetic north, the compass is very helpful for following a heading in the air.

However, have you ever wondered, while turning in the air, what the compass is doing? During a turn it can seem like an eternity for the needle to move on to its new heading; or

Cirro (high cloud) (left and above).

Alto (medium high cloud) (left and above).

Strato (low cloud).

it shoots past and you have to correct your turn. The reason is called 'compass lag' and means quite simply that the part of the compass which points north is slightly heavier than the rest, so during a turn it will have to play catch up or slow down.

So, during a turn in flight, if you are turning from north to south, allowance has to be made for compass lag: undershoot north, overshoot south, UNOS.

Most compasses are filled with white spirit, which enables the moving parts to keep lubricated and working. All compasses have a 'lubber line' that registers the direction in which the aircraft is travelling, in relation to magnetic north. To alter the direction, think of the lubber line as the tail of the aircraft so, turning from north to west, the tail of the aircraft has to move east and turning from south to east the tail of the aircraft has to move west, and so on.

Compasses are affected by electrical items such as GPS, radios, headsets and other electrical instruments, so keep such items well away from the compass during flight. Compasses are also affected by increasing and decreasing airspeed, albeit slightly.

So, if you are heading east to west and you increase you airspeed sharply, you will have an apparent turn to the south, if you decrease your airspeed abruptly heading in the same direction you will have an apparent turn to the north. The opposite applies if you are heading west to east. This is due to the design of the compass: the portion of the compass that points to the north is trying to stay pointing to the north; by increasing or decreasing the airspeed it is just trying to stay pointed at its objective.

CROSSWINDS

On the chart overleaf, the red lines represent the angle of the wind relative to the runway. If the wind is reported as 360 degrees at 20kt and the runway orientation is 340 degrees, the difference is 20 degrees. If you follow the 20-degree line, you will see that the headwind component is 18kt and the crosswind component is 6kt.

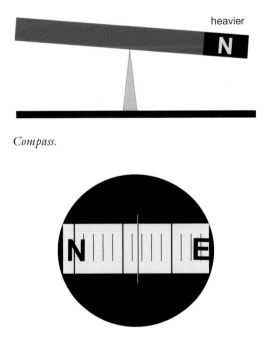

Compass.

Compass lubber.

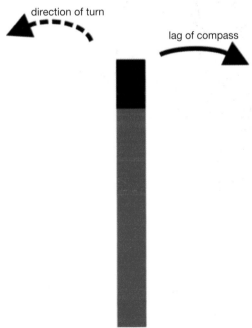

Compass lag.

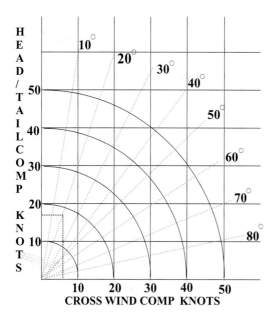

Crosswind relative to runway.

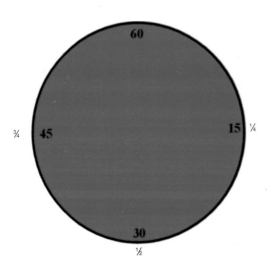

Clock crosswind.

This chart shows that if the wind is 15 degrees off the runway, a quarter of the wind speed is a crosswind component, if it is 30 degrees off then half of it is a crosswind, and so on.

DIFFERENTIAL AILERONS

Differential ailerons are designed so that the up-going aileron rises to a greater angle than the down-going aileron. When we use ailerons we want the plane to roll only on its longitudinal axis. The problem is that to raise a wing the aileron increases lift on that wing with a resultant increase in drag; at the same time there usually is a decreased lift on the opposite wing with a decrease in drag.

DIHEDRAL

Dihedral is what creates stability in roll. Most aircraft, if viewed from the front, will be seen to have wings that are higher at the tips than at the root: this is known as dihedral, and most aircraft have a differing angle, known as the angle of dihedral.

Dihedral works like this: in turbulent air a wing may drop, and as it drops it will tend to slip in the direction of the drop. This has the effect of a crosswind component in the airflow, in relation to the wing (*opposite page, top*).

As the airflow meets the wing, the lower wing meets the airflow at a greater angle of attack than the upper one, and so provides increased lift: this moves the wing back into level flight (*opposite page, bottom*).

DRAG

This is the force that opposes thrust and, therefore, forward movement. Drag varies with airspeed and with the angle of attack of the wing. Drag is apparent in two distinct forms: parasitic drag and induced drag.

Induced Drag

This is linked with the generation of lift. The way the angle of attack of the aerofoil (wing section) meets the airflow causes an upward

Dihedral 1.

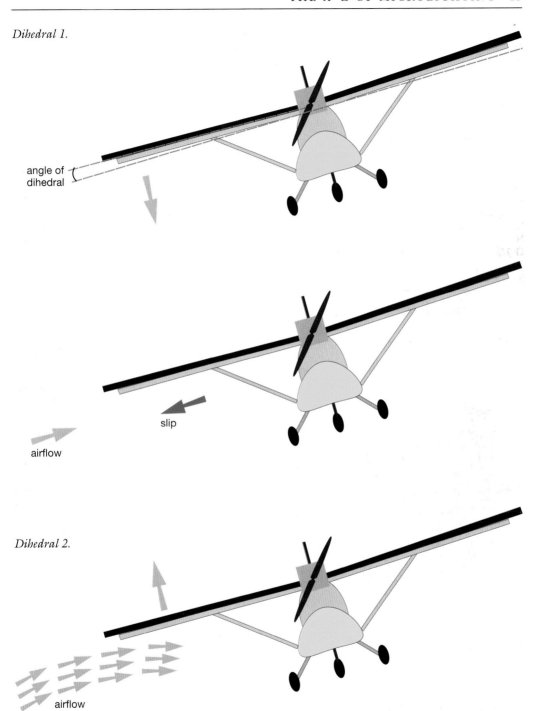

Dihedral 2.

force, acting at right angles to this downward flow to be bent back out of the vertical and at once produces two components.

The vertical component is lift; the horizontal one, which acts rearwards, is induced drag. The greater the angle of attack, the greater the induced drag, so at lower airspeeds we incur more induced drag.

Parasitic Drag

There are many things that will generate air resistance to oppose thrust: the aircraft, the pilot, and so on. This is known as parasitic drag, and as it is caused by air resistance it will increase with an increase in airspeeds.

Total Drag

This is the relationship between airspeed and drag, and is shown in the diagram (*bottom*).

You will see from the diagram that at low airspeeds induced drag has more of an effect while parasitic drag has a lesser effect, and vice versa at higher airspeeds. The total drag curve is depicted in green, showing that drag occurs

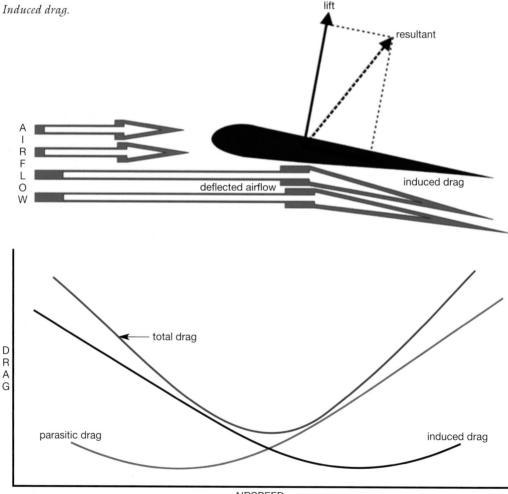

Induced drag.

Drag curves.

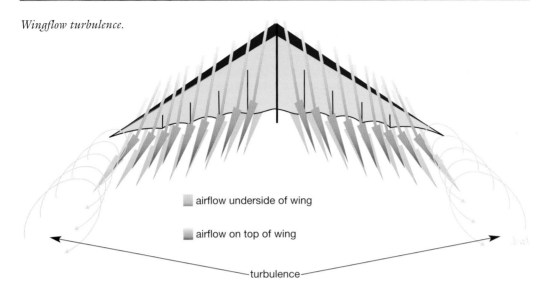

Wingflow turbulence.

airflow underside of wing

airflow on top of wing

turbulence

at both ends of the speed scale: at somewhere in the mid-range drag is at its lowest.

Wing-Tip Vortices

Because in normal flight the pressure is lower on the top of the wing than on the underside, the increased pressure on the underside tries to equalize with the lower pressure on the top. It does this at the wingtips, creating wingtip vortices, or induced drag.

DRIFT

In an ideal world, where there is no wind, no turbulence and no restricted airspace, a line could be drawn on a chart, then that route flown with no problems. However, in the real world we have to contend with drift.

The easiest analogy to explain drift is a fast-moving river. Imagine you are standing on one side, your money is on the other side, it is miles to the nearest bridge and the only way across is to swim: should you jump in and swim toward your money, you would drift downstream.

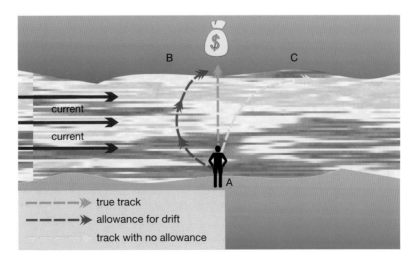

Drift.

B

C

current

current

A

true track

allowance for drift

track with no allowance

Line 'A', to the money, is the true track; 'A' to 'C' is the track with drift not allowed for; 'A' to 'B' is the 'track made good', that is allowing for the drift. The air acts in the same manner as water: the wind affects any aircraft in the air. A tailwind will increase our groundspeed, a headwind will decrease our groundspeed and a crosswind will blow us off track.

DRY ADIABATIC LAPSE RATE (DALR)

When a parcel of air is forced to rise within the atmosphere by whatever means – over hills or mountains, or by uneven heating – the pressure will decrease and with it the temperature. This form of cooling is known as adiabatic cooling. There are fixed rates for dry air and saturated air: dry air cools at 3°C for every 1,000ft it ascends, and saturated air cools at 1.5°C for every 1,000ft it ascends.

Many people think that dry air only occurs on dry days in the summer, but actually dry air may contain moisture: it will only become saturated air when it reaches the point at which the air can condense and form cloud. There is an analogy to explain this that most people have experienced. If you have been swimming on a hot sunny day and then lie on a sun bed, while there you feel distinctly cool: the reason is evaporation, which uses up heat, hence the cooling effect.

There is one other lapse rate that needs to be mentioned, this is the environmental lapse rate (ELR), which varies from day to day.

If the environmental lapse rate is greater than the dry adiabatic lapse rate, then the dry air will continue to rise and the conditions are said to be unstable. If the environmental lapse rate is less than the dry adiabatic lapse rate, then the dry air cannot rise any further and the conditions are said to be stable. The point of equilibrium on the diagram (*below*) is where the air has equalled in temperature and reached its dewpoint, where it will condense into cloud.

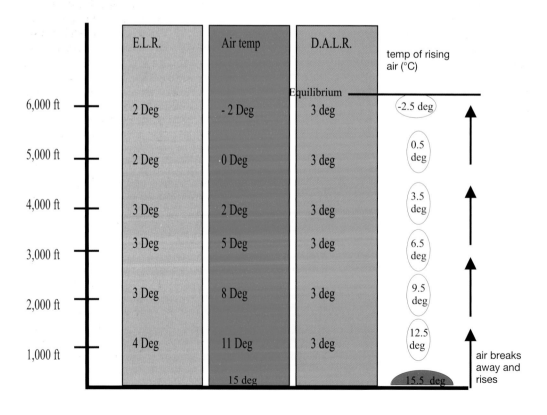

EGO

Don't fall for the oldest trick in the book: 'My mates are going; okay, they have 200 more hours than me, the weather is marginal, but it'll be okay.' Peer pressure is a bug that bites all of us at some stage in our flying career.

'There are old pilots, and there are bold pilots, but there are no old, bold pilots' is an aviation adage that is as old as flying itself.

As I have said above, we satisfy an urge to fly: facing new skills and learning new skills is challenging and healthy, but when our ego gets the better of us, that is when problems can arise. Knowing your limitations is also conducive to healthy living, especially where flying is concerned. Self-discipline and ego are in many ways linked. Sometimes the flying ability of club pilots is wrongly judged by their ability to throw an aircraft around the sky. Trained aerobatics pilots know their stuff, having been thoroughly trained and being conversant with their aircraft.

If you haven't flown for a few weeks, have a check ride with an instructor – most clubs do insist on this anyway, but do it for your own good. The average club pilot flies approximately twelve hours per year; ask yourself whether, if a driver drove his car that rarely, would he be a good driver?

EQUILIBRIUM

Equilibrium is the term we use to explain a constant height and a constant airspeed in which lift = weight and thrust = drag. Equilibrium assumes straight and level flight at a constant airspeed.

EYES

Many believe that microlight pilots are better pilots, mainly because they use their main sensory attribute, their eyes, to their fullest extent.

lift = weight and thrust = drag

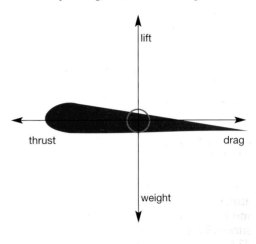

About 80 per cent of our total information intake is through the eyes, so the eye is our prime means of identifying what is happening around us. Simple everyday things can affect our vision, such as dust, fatigue, emotion, age, alcohol and medication. It can also be affected by glare from the sun, and windshields. If you wear glasses for flying, it is a legal requirement that you carry a spare pair with you while flying.

The eye needs time to adjust to a change in the distance over which it is looking: adjusting from an instrument panel 18in away to an object 2 miles away can take up to two or three seconds – remember that when you need ten seconds to avoid a mid-air collision.

We need to see items in binocular vision, and if this is obscured then that is what is known as a 'blind spot', hence the need to move your head while on the lookout (scanning).

The eye has two distinct types of light-sensitive cells, cones and rods. The cones occupy a small central area of the retina. They perceive colours and shapes; they work well in daylight but at night time they become inactive, at which point vision is taken over by the rods.

The rods make up the rest of the retina. They provide peripheral vision during the daylight hours, but there is a problem in that they cannot distinguish colour and they aren't as good at recognizing shapes as the cones. Rods take about thirty minutes to reach their effectiveness, when it is dark. They are also insensitive to red light.

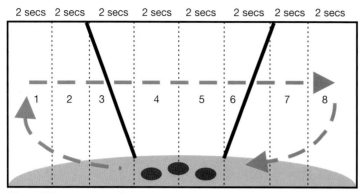

side-to-side scanning technique

Scanning techniques.

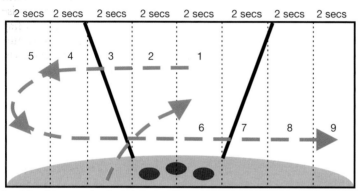

front-to-side scanning technique

So at night, or in very poor visibility, there is an area in the centre of the retina that cannot see anything. This explains, if you have ever done it, why if you look straight at a star you cannot see it, but if you look to the side of it by, say, 10 degrees, you can.

Section of eye.

Cones and rods.

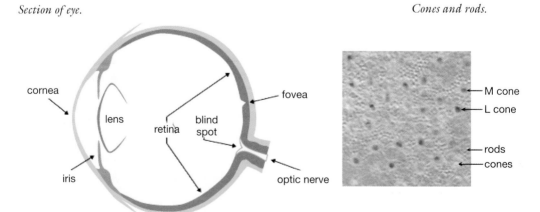

FATIGUE

All of us at some time will be affected by stress or fatigue. The important thing is to recognize how each can affect our flying skills. The aftermath of a family argument is not a good time to go down the airfield, pull the plane out and then bash round the circuit: you will be preoccupied and your concentration will be wavering.

Everyone has stress – yes, everyone! Without it we would be hard-pressed to wake up, never mind get out of bed in the morning. The problem with stress is how each individual deals with it. Sleep disturbance and a poor appetite are both symptoms of stress.

Short-term fatigue is what we experience after strenuous physical exercise and, yes, sex can be considered a short-term exercise. It can be associated with sleepiness, especially after a meal, but can also be the cause of lapses of concentration and the like.

Medium- to long-term fatigue is more associated with shift work, jet lag or just cutting back on sleep – late nights and early mornings. This is the sort of fatigue that causes drivers to fall asleep at the wheel. There is no instant cure, but you need to recognize the symptoms and get adequate rest before a flight.

The acronym I use before I fly is:

I   Illness: am I okay to fly, do I feel good?
M   Medication: am I on any medication that could affect my performance?
S   Stress: am I stressed in any way?
A   Alcohol: 'eight hours bottle to throttle'?
F   Fatigue: am I tired, do I need sleep?
E   Eating: food provides energy

FIN

Sharks have them, dolphins have them and so do aircraft. The fin gives directional stability, direction being controlled by the rudder that is attached to it – yaw control.

The vertical fin gives directional control by keeping the fuselage aligned with the airflow, and it also counterbalances the side area that results from dihedral. If the fin is too small the aircraft will show a coupled rolling, yawing flight path known as 'Dutch Roll'. If the fin is too big, it will overpower the dihedral and cause a spiral dive.

FLAPS

The safest landing is one that can be made at the lowest airspeed and the shortest ground roll. Maximum lift for minimum airspeed can be obtained from the aerofoil, but the form (parasitic) drag hampers the descent cruise speed. There are many differing types of flap configurations, but they all have the same purpose: to increase lift and drag at low airspeeds. Below are a few examples:

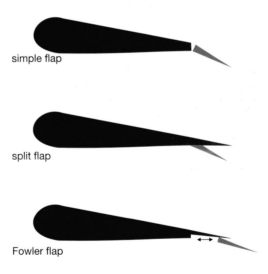

simple flap

split flap

Fowler flap

Rag and tube microlight aircraft generally have simple flaps or flapperons, (flaps and ailerons combined).

FLIGHT RULES

Just as cars and other vehicles on the road have the Highway Code, there are rules and signals in the air that have to be obeyed.

Low-Flying Rules

The general public soon notice a low-flying aircraft. If the low-flying aircraft is a micro-light, this generally leads to a dislike of micro-lights, be it envy or just plain annoyance. The low-flying rules are as follows:

a) An aircraft shall not fly closer than 500ft to any person, vessel, vehicle or structure. Exceptions are:

- Taking off and landing
- Gliders while slope soaring
- Performance at an aircraft race
- Display where the appropriate permission has been obtained.

b) An aircraft other than a helicopter shall not fly over a congested area such as a city, town or settlement used mainly for residential, indus-trial, commercial or recreational purposes:

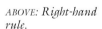

- Below a height that would allow it to land clear of the area without danger to people or property in the event of an engine fail-ure; or
- At less than 1,500ft above the highest fixed object within 2,000ft.

Whichever is the higher. Exceptions to this rule are:

- Taking off and landing
- Flying on a SVFR flight.

c) At a gathering of more than 1,000 people no aircraft shall fly over that gathering or with-in 3,000ft of it. Exceptions to this rule are:

- When flying with the appropriate permis-sion of the authority
- When en route at a reasonable height and in no way associated with the gathering (you could still be reported on this count but your defence would be good if you could prove no connection with the assembly).

Do note that the 500ft rule is not a height stipulation, it is a 'distance from' rule. This is often misunderstood by the public when complaining.

Right-Hand Rule

Position 1: aircraft 2 must give way to the air-craft on the right (aircraft 1)
Position 2: aircraft 2 gives way by a turn to the right, passing behind aircraft 1, keeping it in view to the left
Position 3: aircraft 1 and 2 continue clear of each other

ABOVE: *Right-hand rule.*

Right-hand rule when approaching head-on.

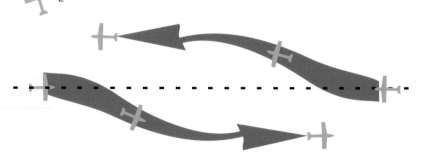

Approaching head-on:

- When two aircraft are approaching head-on, or nearly so, each must turn right
- When following a line feature on the ground, such as a river or a motorway or a railtrack, keep the feature on your left, or keep to the right of the feature.

Ground Signals

See diagrams to the right.

FOG

Advection fog is caused when a warm air mass moves over a colder surface, and is most prevalent at sea. If such a warm air mass moves over colder seas, the lower levels of the air mass are cooled and then condense into fog banks. These fog banks normally disperse on contact with land, because the warmer land evaporates the fog bank back into water vapour. If the land is as cold as the sea, then the fog will remain.

In the winter the opposite can happen as the sea is normally warmer than the land mass, particularly at night. In these circumstances any fog moving off the land toward the sea will disperse on contact with the sea.

If the strength of the sun is sufficient, fog will burn away after a time. If complete dispersal doesn't happen, the fog may lift and form low stratus cloud. We can predict fog if we know the temperature and the relative humidity.

This signal on the ground, viewed from the air means 'landing prohibited', aerodrome closed.

This signal as viewed from the air means that the manoeuvring area is poor and special care is needed.

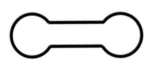

White dumb-bells seen from the air means that the movement of all aircraft is confined to the hard areas only.

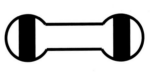

The same dumb-bell outline but with black lines at right angles to the shaft means that only the hard surfaces are to be used for take-offs and landings.

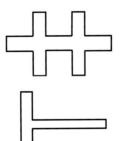

A double white cross denotes gliding in progress.

The direction of take-off and landing is shown by a white 'T'. Land towards the cross-piece of the 'T'.

ABOVE: Airfield markings.

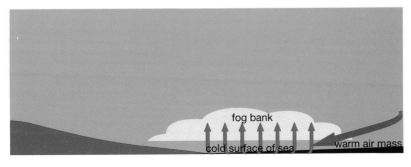

Advection fog.

FORCES

There are four forces at work when an aeroplane is in flight (*see* diagram p.19):

Weight acts vertically downwards (due to gravity) and has to be equalled by a force acting upward so that flight may be continued. Weight doesn't really vary in flight, apart from the small progressive reduction caused by the usage of fuel.

Lift acts upwards to counter weight. Lift varies according to airspeed and to the angle of attack of the aerofoil. Lift acts at 90 degrees to the airflow, but not always in direct opposition to weight when out of straight-and-level flight.

Thrust produces forward movement and provides airflow over the aerofoil. Thrust varies according to the amount of power applied and/or the angle of attack of the aerofoil.

Drag tends to hold back or resist forward movement. The different kinds of drag are described in detail under 'D'. Drag will vary with airspeed and with the angle of attack of the aerofoil.

Lift to drag – at maximum best airspeed.

GLIDE ANGLES

The best glide angle is also the best lift to drag ratio. This is the angle of attack for a given airspeed that produces the most effective lift, with the least drag. Flying at the best glide angle assumes that you will be flying at the best airspeed, which provides the maximum lift to drag ratio. Glide angles are usually expressed as a ratio such as 10:1, which means that for every 10ft that the aircraft travels forwards, it will lose 1ft in height.

You will see from the diagram below that reducing airspeed with the idea of staying aloft longer to cover a greater distance in the glide is not a good one. The increased angle of attack that this brings about might result in an increase in lift, and a reduced rate of sink, but there will also be an increase in drag that will result in a reduction of the lift to drag ratio and so will reduce the distance you can cover in the time you remain in the air.

Increasing airspeed to arrive there before running out of height will not work either. The increase in airspeed requires a reduction in the angle of attack, which also reduces the amount of lift. Although drag reduces as well, the amount is not enough to prevent a reduced lift to drag ratio.

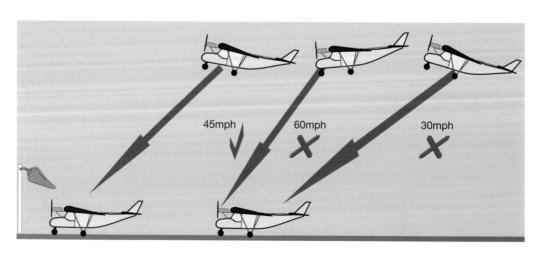

GPS

An affordable, attractive and useful piece of kit, GPS can pinpoint your position to within a few feet and can help keep you clear of busy airspace. Many pilots use them as their main means of navigation, which in principle is fine, until the batteries go down or the unit itself breaks. Many pilots use them in marginal or bad weather as an excuse. 'I will be fine, I have my GPS' – how many times have I heard that? GPS is useful if you are caught out but, again, what happens if it fails?

Charts, as long as they are current, have sufficed for many years, and will continue to do so for a great many more. During training for the pilots licence, no training is given on the use of GPS. You are taught to use a chart, so continue to use a chart and use the GPS as a back-up only.

The basis of GPS is 'triangulation' from satellites. To 'triangulate' a GPS receiver measures distance using the travel time of radio signals. To measure travel time, GPS needs very accurate timing which it achieves with some tricks. Along with distance, it needs to know exactly where the satellites are in space: high orbits and careful monitoring are the secret. Finally, it corrects for any delays the signal experiences as it travels through the atmosphere.

GRADIENTS (WIND)

Friction caused by the ground slows the wind speed at the surface, so there is an increase in wind speed the higher you go. The 'true' wind speed is reached somewhere around 2,000ft. The maximum drop in wind speed occurs very close to the surface and so must be considered carefully before every take-off and, what is more important, landing.

On landing, the effect of wind gradient can be critical. Imagine you are descending on the approach prior to touch-down and you enter a zone of reduced wind speed near the ground. You would feel the aircraft 'sink' very rapidly and might be tempted to raise the nose to stop the sink – DON'T! What is happening is this: your airspeed has temporarily dropped due to the wind gradient, and should you be

ABOVE: GPS – five satellites pinpoint UK position.

Wind gradients.

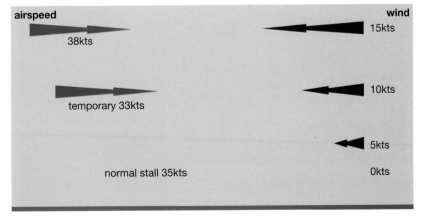

close to stall speed at that time a stall may occur, especially if you raise the nose and so increase the angle of attack (*see* diagram previous page). Be ready with the power, always assume there is wind gradient and there is going to be 'sink'; that way it won't catch you out.

GROUNDSPEED

You will see from the two diagrams below that a headwind reduces groundspeed and a tailwind increases groundspeed:

- A journey of 75nm with a tailwind of 15kt, will take 60 minutes at a constant airspeed of 60kt
- The same journey into a headwind of the same speed would take 1 hour 40 minutes at a constant airspeed of 60kt.

Crosswinds must create a headwind or tailwind 'component', which must be borne in mind when calculating timings for flights. If the wind is behind you even marginally, then your groundspeed will be higher than your airspeed; if, conversely, you have a headwind component then your groundspeed will be less than your airspeed.

Headwind.

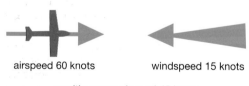

airspeed 60 knots   windspeed 15 knots

resulting groundspeed 45 knots

Tailwind.

windspeed 15 knots   airspeed 60 knots

resulting groundspeed 75 knots

HANG-GLIDER

The hang-glider was originally developed by a NASA scientist to recover the Gemini space craft. It was named the 'Rogallo' wing after the NASA scientist who developed it, Francis Rogallo.

Hang-gliding is a freedom sport: to be able to fly, all you need is a hill, cliff or other launch area, a hang-glider and, of course, some tuition. Soaring is one of the most pleasurable experiences to be had in aviation, but sometimes conditions do not permit extended flight, hence the development of the powered hang-glider.

HILL LIFT

Hill lift is associated with soaring. Wind, or too much of it, can be our enemy, but there are times when it can be a friend. If you should talk to hang-glider pilots and ask them about hill lift, they usually wax lyrical about its benefits.

The illustration (*above right*) explains hill lift. The left-hand picture depicts how the wind follows the contour of any given hill, and the right-hand picture depicts the breakdown of the forces:

R The resultant caused by the hill
H The horizontal component of that resultant
V The vertical component of that resultant and the one that is most important in hill lift

The best area for hill lift is to be found about one-third out from the top in relation to the foot of the hill. It has huge benefits to the microlight pilot, who can use that lift to remain airborne for long periods without using too much fuel.

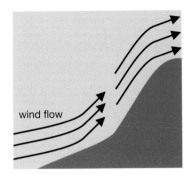

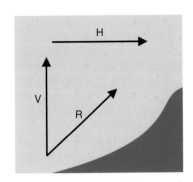

Hill lift.

BELOW: Hoar frost.

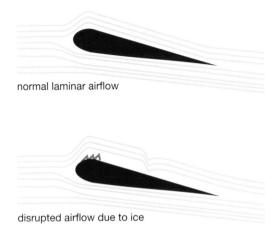

normal laminar airflow

disrupted airflow due to ice

HOAR FROST

We have all dealt with hoar frost at some time in our lives: the ice you scrape from your car windscreen on a frosty morning is hoar frost. Hoar frost can have a devastating effect on the performance of the aircraft as it can disrupt the smooth airflow over the aerofoil section, inhibiting lift. It can develop while the aircraft is parked on the ground, or even while

descending from a freezing level to warmer, moister air. Remove all traces from all surfaces before any flight.

Ice needs a freezing nuclei to be present to form. The process of water vapour transforming into ice crystals is known as deposition, and without the presence of these freezing nuclei water can remain in a liquid state well under 0°C. These are then known as super-cooled water droplets and usually turn to ice on striking an object.

HUMIDITY

Humidity affects the density of the air: if the air has a high water content, it will be less dense than drier air. Relative humidity is the measurement of water vapour present in a given mass of air, normally expressed as a percentage of the total amount of water vapour that that mass could hold before becoming saturated.

Temperature has a bearing on the amount of water vapour the air can hold, as illustrated below. If a mass of air, at a given temperature, contains 50 per cent of the total water vapour that it could hold, its relative humidity is 50 per cent (A).

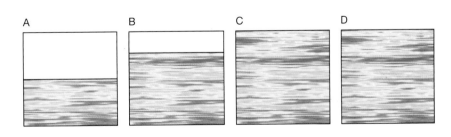

A   B   C   D

Humidity.

When this air is cooled, it can contain less water vapour, so the same water vapour increases in amount, relative to the maximum amount of such vapour that the mass of the air can hold (B).

If the air cools further, the water vapour content can eventually reach the point where the air is only just able to contain it. This mass of air is now considered saturated, with a relative humidity of 100 per cent: this is known as the dewpoint (C).

If the air cools further still, it will produce more water vapour than the air can hold. At this point condensation can take place, where the excess invisible water vapour converts into water particles as cloud. If this occurs at ground level, it will form dew or fog (D). For any condensation to take place, there must be present, minute particles of matter, such as dust in the atmosphere – these are known as condensation nuclei.

HYPERVENTILATION

Commonly known as 'over breathing', hyperventilation is the exhalation of more carbon dioxide than is necessary in the normal breathing process. The signs of hyperventilation are: tingling at the extremities, hot/cold feeling anywhere in the body, vision clouded or tunnelled. If this occurs in the air, treat as hypoxia unless you are below 10,000ft.

HYPOXIA

The air we breathe is made up of:

- 78 per cent nitrogen
- 21 per cent oxygen
- 1 per cent other gases (including carbon dioxide, argon and water vapour).

These percentages remain the same throughout the atmosphere. What changes is the amount of pressure, which decreases as we ascend. To a fit person the effect of a lack of oxygen, hypoxia, will not normally make itself felt below 10,000ft, though it can start to tell at 8,000ft if you are feeling ill. The symptoms of hypoxia

are as follows:

- Judgment becomes sloppy with a pilot unaware that his/her performance is lacking: decisions are made at a slower speed, coordination is affected
- The senses – touch, vision and hearing – all become affected; there can also be personality changes, from aggression to being 'slap happy'
- All this time consciousness is dropping away and death can result if remaining at high altitudes and with no supplementary oxygen.

Hypoxia is accelerated by smoking, alcohol, moving around, feeling ill, long periods of exposure and higher altitudes.

ICING (CARBURETTOR)

When pressure decreases, so does temperature. When evaporation takes place, temperature drops. In a carburettor the decrease in pressure is bought about by the Venturi effect (*see* below); this, coupled with the evaporation of fuel as it enters the airflow, can give a sharp drop in temperature, which can be as much as 33°C in a fraction of a second.

If the drop in temperature takes the carburettor below 0°C, then any water particles produced by condensation will turn at once into ice. The ice can build up in amounts sufficient to restrict the intake of fuel mixture into the cylinder so that not only can power be reduced, but there could be an engine failure.

Carburettor icing is most prevalent when the air is moist and the temperature is between –7°C and +21°C. In the UK this is practically any time, but most carburettor icing occurs when the engine is at a low power setting, such as during a glide descent. Carburettor icing is more likely if Mogas fuel is used, because of its higher water content.

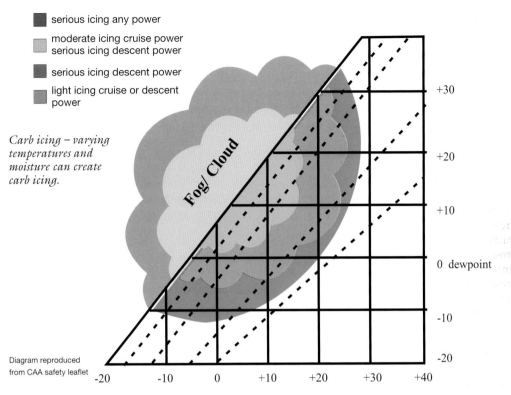

- ■ serious icing any power
- □ moderate icing cruise power
  serious icing descent power
- ■ serious icing descent power
- ■ light icing cruise or descent power

Carb icing – varying temperatures and moisture can create carb icing.

Diagram reproduced from CAA safety leaflet

Venturi Effect

Imagine a hose pipe with water flowing through it. If you stood on the hose pipe the water would still come through, but at the point where your foot is compressing the pipe the water must be travelling at a greater speed due to the restriction. Due to the increased speed of the water, the pressure it can exert on the walls of the pipe is less. The same happens to a mass of air passing through a carburettor.

The chart (*bottom*) shows the wide range of ambient conditions where the formation of carburettor icing is most likely. Note a much greater risk of serious icing with descent power. The closer the temperature and dewpoint readings, the greater the relative humidity.

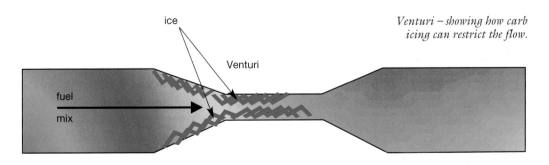

Venturi – showing how carb icing can restrict the flow.

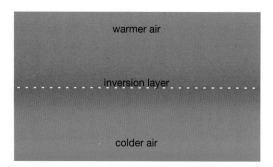

Inversions.

INTERNATIONAL STANDARD ATMOSPHERE (ISA)

ISA is the standard setting to which all instruments are calibrated:

Pressure	1,013.25Mb*
Temperature at sea level	15°C
Density	1,225g/m³
Average lapse rate	1.98°C per 1,000ft

* *The ISA altimeter setting is 1,013.2Mb as most altimeters cannot be set to hundredths of a millibar.*

INVERSIONS

An inversion is a situation in which temperature increases with height. This is usually the result of warm air (which is less dense than cold) climbing over colder air. Inversions can occur near the ground, when the ground cools rapidly in the evening through radiation and the air in contact with the ground is colder than that above. Inversions are noted for trapping haze and fog, and causing bad visibility.

ISOBARS

Isobars indicate airflow or air movement. Many isobars on a weather map – such as those you might see on television – indicate strong winds, and fewer or no isobars indicate light winds or no wind at all. Isobars also indicate lines of equal air pressure.

Isobars.

The chart (*above*) shows that it is reasonably windy across the UK, but more so across Ireland and the south-west of the UK.

JOINING THE CIRCUIT

When a flight is nearing its completion, be it at your own airfield or the one you are visiting, you will need to join the circuit with the intention of landing. Different airfields have differing procedures, so you must check with the airfield you intend to fly to for their particular joining preferences. Here I will cover the joining procedures that are mostly used.

The overhead join is the one most pilots opt for when approaching an airfield. Generally you will arrive overhead the airfield at 2,000ft QFE. This means that you have set the 'field elevation' on your altimeter, and are 2,000ft

Live- and deadsides.

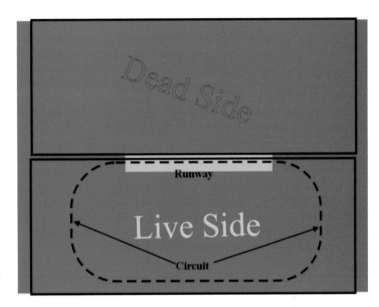

BELOW: Always descend on the deadside.

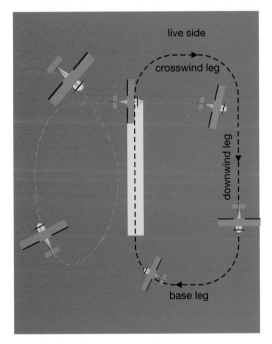

above the airfield. The airfield is split into two different sections: a liveside, where all activity exists for the circuit; and a deadside, where all descents are carried out.

I am assuming that you have radio contact with your destination airfield and that you have informed them of your intentions. Having done that, you can then start your descent down to circuit height, making sure that you descend on the deadside.

When you have descended to the desired circuit height, which for these purposes we will assume to be 700ft QFE, you must make sure you have ended up in the correct position to then join the circuit. Generally you would join the circuit on the downwind leg (*see* illustration *left*).

So, from 2,000ft you would descend on the deadside until you reached the prescribed circuit height; then you would fly on a crosswind heading, passing over the threshold of the runway, and then join the circuit on the downwind leg. From then on you fly a normal circuit.

THE JOINT AVIATION AUTHORITY (JAA)

The JAA is not really an issue with microlights in the UK, but it is worth knowing what it is. European harmony in aviation procedures is taking place under the auspices of the JAA, which makes recommendations to the European Commission in Brussels. By contrast, microlighting bodies in most countries are maintaining their national identity.

KATA FRONTS

Should there be a descending movement in the warm air at a front, the depth to which the cloud extends will be stunted. The front depicted (*opposite page*) is called a 'Kata Warm Front', simply because the warm air is descending.

There can also be a 'Kata Cold Front', as depicted (*opposite page*), again simply because the warm air is descending. This leads us nicely into katabatic winds (*below?*). Anything prefixed with 'kata' in weather-talk means 'down' and anything preffixed 'ana' means 'up'.

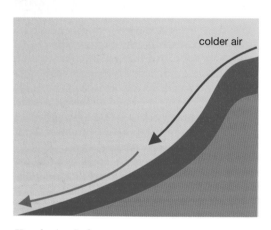

Katabatic winds.

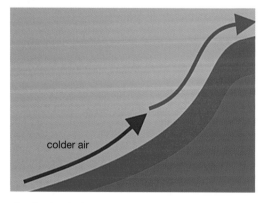

Anabatic winds.

KATABATIC WINDS

Colder air from the tops of mountains or large hills rolls down the slopes – as a result of it being more dense than the warm air below – into the lower ground of the valleys; this phenomenon is more frequent at night. When this cold air meets the warmer valley air, mists can appear through convection: these are called advection fogs. *See also* 'Valley Winds'.

During the day the reverse happens, anabatic winds being the opposite of katabatic winds. These winds flow up the slopes of mountains from the valleys as the radiational warming of the lower slopes and valleys causes air to rise. An anabatic wind is also named a 'valley breeze'. Anabatic winds are typically daytime winds during the summer.

KNOTS

A knot is a nautical measure of speed, one nautical mile per hour (about 1.15mph, or 1.85km/h). The name comes from the knots tied in the 'log line' used with the sand glass on board ship. The log line (a line with a log attached to the end, hence the name) was thrown onto the sea and the knots in the line were counted as they ran out during the sand-glass interval. The knot has been used since the seventeenth century and is sometimes called the sea mile. The international knot is very slightly less than the UK knot.

Nautical miles measure distance. One nautical mile is the angular distance of one minute of arc on the earth's surface. As these differ slightly (6108' at the poles, compared with 6046' at the equator), 6080 was adopted (this being its approximate value in the English Channel).

Most but not all microlight aircraft have their airspeed indicators (ASIs) calibrated in miles per hour. This is fine until we want to start working out timings and allowing for the wind speed. Wind speed is measured in knots, so don't forget to convert mph into knots or vice versa, as required. The chart (*opposite*) is a simple conversion chart.

MPH	Knots
10	9
15	13
20	18
25	22
30	26
35	30

MPH	Knots
45	39
50	44
55	48
60	54
65	57
70	61

Simple conversion chart.

BELOW: **Kata fronts.**

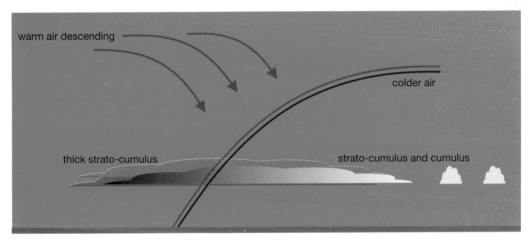

Kata warm front.

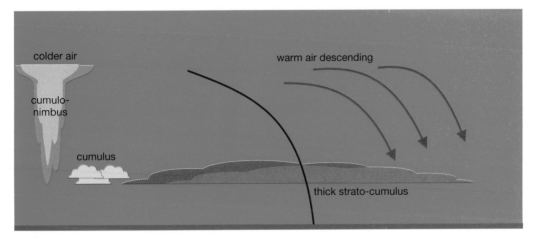

Kata cold front.

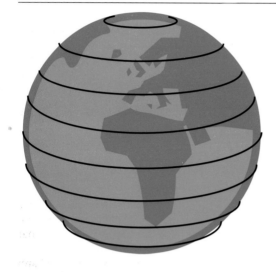

Lines of latitude.

LATITUDE

Latitude lines run horizontally. Latitude lines are also known as parallels since they are parallel; they are also equidistant from each other. Each degree of latitude is approximately 69 miles (111km) apart; there is a variation because the earth is not a perfect sphere but an 'oblate ellipsoid' (slightly egg-shaped). To remember latitude, imagine them as the horizontal rungs of a ladder ('ladder-tude'). Degrees of latitude are numbered from 0 degrees to 90 degrees north and south. Zero degrees is the equator, the imaginary line that divides our planet into the northern and southern hemispheres. Ninety degrees north is the North Pole and 90 degrees south is the South Pole.

LENTICULAR CLOUDS

Lenticular clouds.

BELOW: *The formation of lenticular clouds.*

Winds carrying air over a mountain rise up one side, cooling on the way up so that moisture in the air condenses to form a cloud. When the air moves down the other side of the mountain, it warms up. The droplets in the cloud then turn back to water vapour because warm air can hold more vapour than cool air.

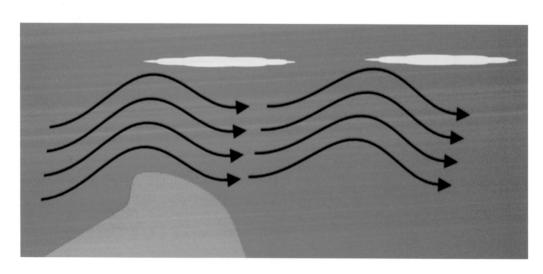

Since winds are constantly blowing over the mountain, the cloud is continually renewed. It therefore appears to remain in position, since it marks the spot where air is cooled into condensation. Lenticular clouds are not always seen over mountains. The airflow must be smooth, rather than turbulent, to allow the beautiful layer-cake structure to develop.

LICENCES

There are two types of licence for a microlight pilot: a restricted licence and a full licence. A restricted licence is obtainable in minimum of fifteen hours' training. If you have a restricted licence you cannot fly:

- When the surface wind is 15 knots or above
- When the cloud base is below 1,000ft
- When the in-flight visibility is below 10km
- Outside a radius of 8nm from your take-off point
- With passengers, unless you have twenty-five hours logged, ten of them as pilot in command, and you have had your logbook endorsed by an examiner to verify those hours.

To lift the restrictions to gain a full licence you must fly a further ten hours under the instruction of an instructor, five of which must be navigation training. You must complete two solo cross-country flights of at least 40nm under the supervision of an instructor; these must be on different routes and each have one land-away point at least 15nm from the take-off point.

Most students aim for the full licence, but the restricted licence is a godsend for those bad winter days when you cannot fly and don't want to loose the validity (for counting toward your licence) of all the hours you have put in and of the ground exams.

LOGBOOK

Personal Flying Record

A personal flying book must be kept by a qualified pilot and by a student under training for the purposes of becoming a qualified pilot. The logbook must be kept available, to be produced to any recognized authority, for a minimum of two years after the date of the last entry.

Flight time according to the Air Navigation Order (ANO) is from the first time the aircraft moves from rest under its own power, for the purposes of undertaking a flight, to engine shutdown after a landing. I slightly disagree with this as it is not clear which part of the aircraft has to move – the key, the pistons, the propeller? Most schools that I know of log their flight times from engine start to engine shutdown, and most Hobbs meters (that show aircraft time) work this way too.

The minimum particulars to be recorded are:

- The date of the flight
- The type of aircraft
- The registration of the aircraft
- Take-off point and landing point
- The name of the pilot in command
- The status of the pilot in flight, i.e. pilot under training, or pilot in charge
- The total flight time
- The details of the activity or training; if a student, this must be signed by an instructor.

Aeroplane Logbooks

Separate logbooks must be kept for the engine and for the airframe, though there are specially designed combination logbooks that will suffice. All incidents, inspections and maintenance must be recorded, along with details of both flying and engine hours.

LONGITUDE

The vertical longitude lines are also known as meridians. They converge at the poles and are widest at the equator (about 69 miles or 111km apart). Zero degrees longitude passes through Greenwich, England. (Greenwich, the site of the British Royal Greenwich Observatory, was established as the site of the Prime Meridian by an international conference in 1884.) The degrees continue 180 degrees east and 180

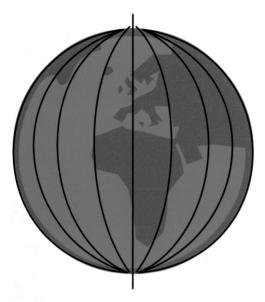

Lines of longitude.

degrees west until they meet and form the International Date Line in the Pacific Ocean.

To precisely locate points on the earth's surface, degrees longitude and latitude have been divided into minutes (') and seconds ("). There are 60 minutes in each degree, and each minute is divided into 60 seconds. Seconds can be further divided into tenths, hundredths, or even thousandths. For example, the centre of Washington, DC, is at 38°53'23"N, 77°00'27"W: this is 38 degrees, 53 minutes, and 23 seconds north of the equator and 77 degrees, 0 minutes and 27 seconds west of the Greenwich meridian.

LOW-LEVEL TURBULENCE

The air in the atmosphere is rarely at rest, especially near the ground. If you need proof of this point, watch smoke rising from a chimney stack: rarely does it go straight up; it falls, lifts and moves around.

If you look at the illustration below, it could be likened to a cross-section of a river. High up (the surface of the river) all looks calm, while near the ground (the river bed) eddies occur, moving faster, moving slower and displacing air. Obstacles will affect the movement of the air – buildings, trees, hills, even mountains.

Uneven heating also plays a large part in providing turbulent conditions. Some surfaces absorb more heat than others and some surfaces give off more heat than others, hence thermal activity. Thermic activity starts as a 'bubble' of air that is warmer than the surrounding air, lying on a heated surface like a soap bubble until it is disturbed upwards. At this point, it will pick up speed until the buoyancy forces balance the drag forces. The thermal contracts initially as it assumes a spherical shape, then expands fairly constantly with height. Thermic activity can have a dramatic effect on approach, as shown in the illustration (*below*).

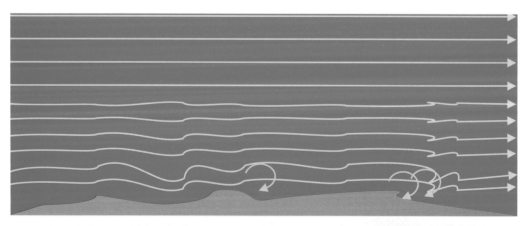

Low-level turbulence.

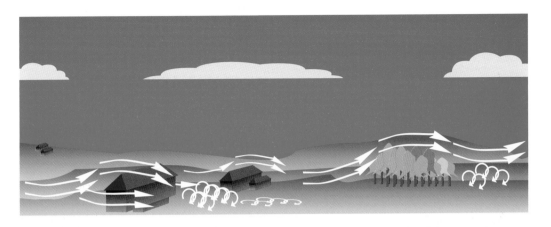

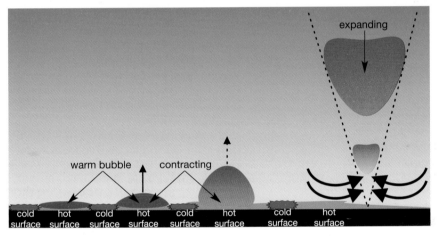

ABOVE: *low-
level
turbulence.
Buildings and
other structures
can have an
effect.*

*The birth of a
thermal.*

Thermic activity can have a dramatic effect on approach.

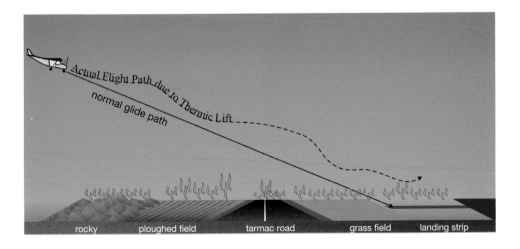

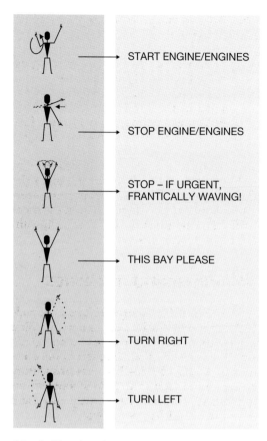

START ENGINE/ENGINES

STOP ENGINE/ENGINES

STOP – IF URGENT, FRANTICALLY WAVING!

THIS BAY PLEASE

TURN RIGHT

TURN LEFT

Marshalling signals. BELOW: *Air masses.*

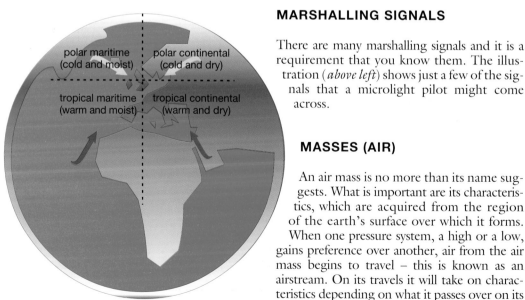

polar maritime (cold and moist)

polar continental (cold and dry)

tropical maritime (warm and moist)

tropical continental (warm and dry)

MAPS (CHARTS)

There are two scales of aviation charts used in UK light aviation, the charts available in each covering all of the UK. The scales used are:

- ¼ million (1:250,000) – 4 statute miles to 1 inch approx.
- ½ million (1:500,000) – 8 statute miles to 1 inch approx.

The scale of chart used mainly by microlight aviators is the ¼ million because, at the heights and speeds at which microlights travel, it enables much more information to be absorbed. The ½ million chart shows the details of all airspace (e.g. control zones), while the ¼ million chart only shows airspace from the surface up to 5,000ft.

It is a legal requirement to carry with you while flying a current chart of the area you are flying in. The information on each chart is well worth absorbing, and it is more interesting than reading umpteen books on the topic.

MARSHALLING SIGNALS

There are many marshalling signals and it is a requirement that you know them. The illustration (*above left*) shows just a few of the signals that a microlight pilot might come across.

MASSES (AIR)

An air mass is no more than its name suggests. What is important are its characteristics, which are acquired from the region of the earth's surface over which it forms.

When one pressure system, a high or a low, gains preference over another, air from the air mass begins to travel – this is known as an airstream. On its travels it will take on characteristics depending on what it passes over on its journey: this is known as transformation. The characteristics it takes depend on what it travels over and how long it takes to travel over it.

If, for example, the air mass moves from the south-west then its characteristics will be warm and moist – *see* the illustration (*below left*).

METAR

METAR stands for METeorological Aerodrome Report. These are issued by civil and military aerodromes to show the actual weather happening at a particular time.

MICROLIGHT

The definition of a microlight in the ANO (currently) is:

- 450kg maximum take-off weight (MTOW) for a two-seat landplane
- 495kg MTOW for a two-seat amphibian or floatplane
- 300kg MTOW for a single-seat landplane
- 330kg MTOW for a single-seat amphibian or floatplane
- Maximum wing loading must not exceed 25kg per square metre

Or

- A stalling speed in level flight not exceeding a calibrated airspeed of 35kt (41mph/65km/h)
- All microlight aeroplanes must be in possession of a noise certificate.

There are two categories of aeroplanes for airworthiness purposes:

- **Type approved**, which are all microlights that first flew after 1 January 1984.
- **Type accepted**, which are all microlights that first flew before 1 January 1984 if over 70kg empty weight, or prior to 1 January 1987 if less than 70kg empty weight.

Type-accepted machines are aeroplanes that were flying before the introduction of legislation, but for which on performance, engineering and track record there has been sufficient evidence to show they can continue to fly without any modifications.

MILITARY AIR TRAFFIC ZONES

A military air traffic zone (MATZ) is an extended ATZ around a military aerodrome, reaching up to 3,000ft above aerodrome level (QFE) within a 5nm radius of the centre of the aerodrome. MATZ do not have any mandatory powers, but entering a MATZ without informing anyone could have dire consequences, and of course the ATZ rules still apply.

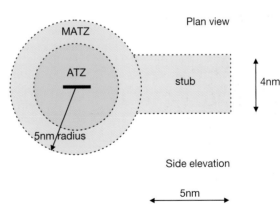

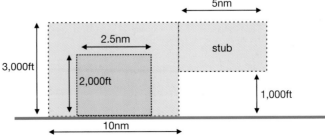

Military Air Traffic Zones.

MILITARY LOW FLYING

Military low flying in the UK takes place from the surface to 2,000ft. This permits a wide distribution of this noisy activity to reduce its environmental impact. Military pilots must avoid major built-up areas, controlled airspace, aerodrome traffic zones and other sensitive locations, such as hospitals.

Having said all that, one incident springs to mind. I was briefing a very early-houred student, who was quite nervous anyway, and we were discussing the low-flying rules. When he asked what would happen if we came face to face with a fast-moving military jet, I said 'We'd have no chance.' After I had calmed him down, I told him that in all the time that I had been at that particular airfield, and I had been there about a year, I hadn't seen a single low-level military aircraft anywhere near the airfield. He accepted what I had said and then he continued outside to check over the aircraft for his flight. Then, at what seemed like 10ft above the ground, a Tornado jet flew over! We both ducked (yes it was *that* low!), we both looked at each other and he nearly burst into tears, saying something like 'That's what I mean.' I replied 'That's a first.' We both laugh about it now, but it just goes to show you that the military can 'pop up' anywhere.

To avoid conflict, it is best to fly above 2,000ft AGL when possible, and in particular to avoid flying between 250 and 1,000ft AGL except when climbing out from/descending into an airfield.

NAVIGATION

Navigation, or the thought of it, fills most pilots with awe: their immediate thought is maps, rulers, protractors, angles, velocities, physics and so on, and so forth. Navigation in the air, if learned correctly, can be a rewarding and very interesting subject. It is broken into two parts:

- Planning a route from A to B (navigation planning)
- Flying that route (map reading).

Compasses

All microlight aircraft have a compass that tells the pilot where he is heading, in relation to magnetic north. You must rely on this instrument if you are going to advance in the field of navigation. However, there is a discrepancy between True North and Magnetic North, called variation. Variation changes, both with time and according to where you are on the earth. Lines joining places of equal variation are called isogonals, and are marked on aeronautical charts by a blue dashed line, running at an angle to the longitudinal lines.

The compass has another complication, which is that the aircraft's own magnetic field acts upon it; this is called deviation. Most microlight aircraft don't have this problem due to the lack of heavy instrumentation and metals in their structure. If your aircraft *does* play havoc with the compass readings, a card is generally placed near the compass at the time of building on which is stated how much deviation you have to apply for that particular aircraft.

All charts are marked and set up using geographical north, so to establish a compass heading there are a few simple calculations to be made. Variation and deviation can be toward either the east or the west, so a ditty was made up to remember the formula:

'Variation west, magnetic best' – add to the true heading

'Variation east, magnetic least' – subtract from the true heading.

The same ditty applies to deviation, but remember that variation is applied to true headings and deviation is applied to magnetic headings.

Route Planning

To plan a route from A to B you will need various items of equipment:

- A ruler, preferably a scaled ruler (one that matches the charts you are using scaled in nautical miles)
- A protractor, to measure the angle of track against the line of longitude on the chart
- A chart, current and covering the area of the intended flight
- Some scrap paper.

The first part of the planning exercise is to decide where you are going! So draw a line on your chart using the ruler, clearly and neatly. (For the purposes of this exercise I will assume you are flying in a straight line from A to B.) Using the protractor, measure your track line in relation to True North, to find the direction in which you will need to travel.

> ERROR CHECK! Make sure you have the map oriented so that north is away from you and south is nearest you.

After you have written down the true track (expressed as degrees), you now need to add or subtract the variation in order to end up with a compass heading. Once that is complete, you may need to do the same with deviation, though for the purposes of this exercise I will disregard deviation as it varies from aircraft to aircraft.

When you have your compass heading, you can now work out the timings: how long it will take you to fly from A to B and therefore your ETA. If you know what airspeed you will be flying at, then the formula is very simple:

$$\frac{\text{Distance of track}}{\text{Airspeed}} = \text{Time}$$

So, let's say distance of track is 60nm and airspeed is 60kt: time = 1 hour A to B.

> ERROR CHECK! Don't forget to work in the same nominations, i.e. nautical miles and knots, or statute miles and mph. They must not be mixed.

Next we need to consider the wind. We rarely have totally still days, in fact more often than not the wind prohibits us from flying at all! The wind has an effect on several different items that affect our flight and the planning of it. It can affect our groundspeed as shown (*below*). This will of course affect our timings. Another influence we may have to contend with is drift.

Headwind.

airspeed 60 knots   windspeed 15 knots

resulting groundspeed 45 knots

Tailwind.

windspeed 15 knots   airspeed 60 knots

resulting groundspeed 75 knots

You will see from the above illustration that wind has a profound effect on flight. If we have a crosswind we have to allow for it, or else we would be blown off course. You have

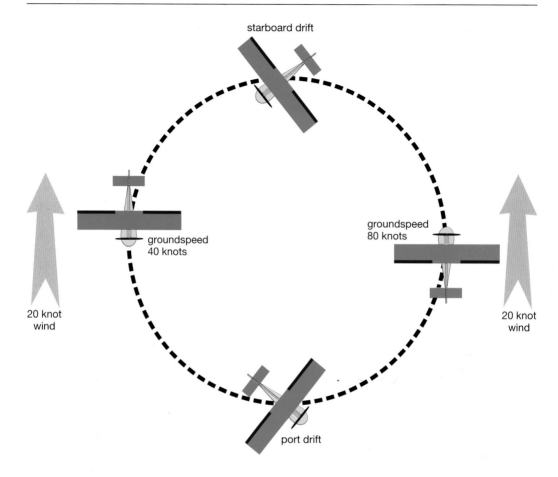

starboard drift

groundspeed
40 knots

groundspeed
80 knots

20 knot
wind

20 knot
wind

port drift

Drift – assuming a 60kt airspeed.

to point the nose of the aircraft into the wind to counteract the effect of the crosswind.

To work out the exact adjustment we have to draw three vectors and form a triangle of velocities. Each vector is comprised of a velocity (a speed and a direction) related to the flight. We should always know two of the vectors, so given that we can work out the third.

Route Planning – Example

Let's go through an example of planning a flight. I will assume that you have drawn a line on your chart from your departure point A to destination point B, measured the distance of the track, and measured the angle of the track in relationship to true north. From your chart

you would have gained the following information: track required is 215 degrees (T). From the weather report you would have gained the following information: the wind is 140 degrees at 15kt. Information that you would already have is: true airspeed (TAS), 60kt. The two unknowns are: the heading (T) to counteract the wind drift and the ground-speed that results from the wind effect. Step by step, the planning process is as follows:

1. With a ruler draw a vertical line on your scrap piece of paper, to represent a line of longitude. Then, using the protractor, lay off a line to represent your track line at 215 degrees. Your drawing should now look like the one in Step 1 (*opposite*).

Route planning –
Step 1.

Route planning –
Step 2.

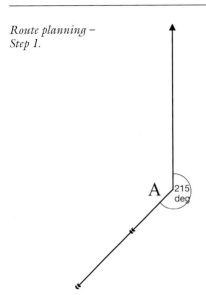

Route planning – Step 3.

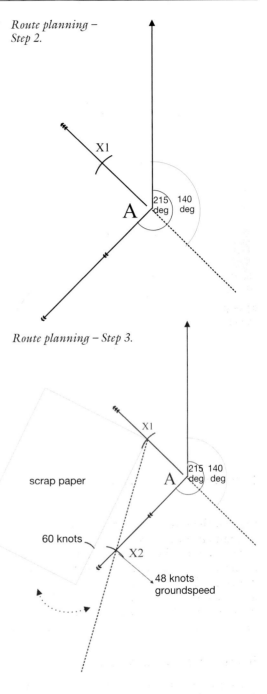

2. Lay off a 'wind line' at 140 degrees, downwind from the start point 'A'. Mark this line with three arrows so as not to confuse it with the others. Now select a scale that is large enough to allow accuracy but small enough to fit your workspace, to depict the 15kt wind vector; measure this along the wind line and mark it off 'x1'.

3. Next, to show the 60kt true airspeed vector, use another scrap of paper and measure '60kt' off from one corner, along one edge in the same scale you are using. Place the corner of the paper on the x1 mark and rotate the paper until it intersects with the track line at 'x2'; when it does, mark that point on the line A–B. The length of that line from A to x2 represents the actual groundspeed, so using the same scale, read off groundspeed, which in this case is 48kt.

ERROR CHECK! If you have a head wind, your groundspeed should be lower than your airspeed, and vice versa if you have a tailwind.

4. Finally, parallel the line 'x1 to x2' so that it passes through point 'A' and then measure the angle. This will be your new heading allowing for the wind factor (drift) to maintain your true track. In this case it is 198 degrees (the red line).

Route planning – Step 4.

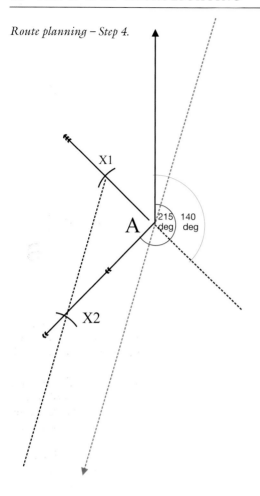

You should have now successfully calculated the two unknowns, groundspeed and heading allowing for the wind, so you can now go on to complete the planning by working out the timings. Distance of track divided by groundspeed = time. So 60nm divided by 48kt = 75 minutes flying time.

FINAL ERROR CHECK! Make sure you are using the same units for airspeed and windspeed; the heading and the wind arrows should always be following each other around the triangle; the heading should always be less than the track required, because adjustment is always made into wind of track.

Next you will have to apply variation and deviation (if required) to end up with a compass reading.

Wandering Off Course

So you have planned your route, you are on your way, you are following your compass heading correctly, but all of a sudden the chart doesn't fit the mental picture: 'That river should be on my left, not my right', 'Is that this town, or is it that town?'

Because of the simplicity of microlights, their slow airspeeds (although they are getting quicker) and their ability to land almost anywhere to check where you are, getting lost isn't really an option. After all, as a Red Arrows' pilot once said to me, and I quote, 'You aren't lost, until you're lost at Mach 2.'

Following a track line on a chart is a reasonably simple matter, assuming that you can fly an aircraft reasonably competently, but things can and do go wrong:

• The wind is stronger than forecast
• Your planning is all wrong
• The compass is malfunctioning ... hmm!

More than likely you were enjoying yourself so much that you have inadvertently wandered slightly off-course, but dangers could lie ahead, such as controlled airspace and the like.

There is a simple method to make sure that you don't wander too much off track. It has to be done right at the start of the planning stage and involves drawing fan lines on your chart (*opposite page, top*). This method is called the 10-degree rule and requires no advanced mathematical calculations.

Let us suppose that after a time you realize that you are off track and you have noted your position by reference to a feature on the ground that corresponds to your chart – basically, you know where you are!

You have to make an educated estimate of how far you are off your original track – let's say you estimate yourself to be 7 degrees starboard (right) of track. A change of 7 degrees to port (left) will simply result in a parallel track. However, you can see that you are 5 degrees off track from the destination fan line,

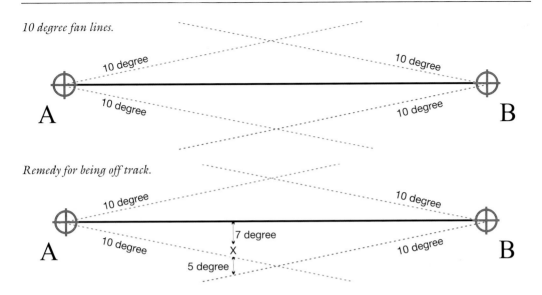

10 degree fan lines.

Remedy for being off track.

so simply add the two together: 7 degrees + 5 degrees = 12 degrees to port. This should see you safely to your destination.

OROGRAPHIC CLOUD FORMATION

Cloud is formed by cooling a mass of air until it can reach its dewpoint. Air, on meeting large hills and mountains, obviously has to rise to pass over them; as it does so it will cool adiabatically. If the dewpoint is reached it will condense.

The main type of cloud that is formed this way is stratiform cloud in the form of stratus or stratocumulus, if the conditions are stable. Any cloud that forms below the top of a hill is designated as hill fog.

The other type of orographic cloud is cumiliform cloud, which is formed if the conditions are unstable and convection is triggered off by the rising air (*see* the illustrations, p.46).

Orographic cloud formation.

Orographic cloud.

Orographic cloud forming.

OXYGEN

Oxygen is the most common element by volume or mass (weight) on Earth. In each breath you take, one-fifth of the molecules are oxygen; there are twelve trillion tons of oxygen in the air. Yet although it is so common, we are hardly aware of this vital element because oxygen is transparent, it has no colour, taste or smell.

Oxygen in the Air

Air is a gas made up chiefly of nitrogen and oxygen. Oxygen (O_2) makes up 21 per cent of the atmosphere by volume and 23 per cent by mass. The weight of oxygen molecules in the atmosphere helps to create the air pressure on the Earth's surface, which averages 1kg on every cm^2.

Although ozone (O_3) is only present in concentrations as little as 12 parts per million, it is present both in the upper atmosphere and close to the ground.

The composition of clean air:

- 78 per cent nitrogen
- 21 per cent oxygen
- 1 per cent other gases (including carbon dioxide, argon and water vapour).

Orographic cap cloud.

PERMIT TO FLY

All microlight aircraft must have a current Permit to Fly in order to fly legally in the UK. The permit is renewed annually, subject to a satisfactory inspection by an approved inspector and then a flight by an approved check pilot, usually the same person. The inspection must be carried out against a laid-down schedule and any specific documents pertinent to the aircraft type. Most Permits to Fly contain the following criteria:

- A microlight aircraft may not be used for the purposes of public transport or aerial work, other than work consisting of the giving of instruction in flying where the aircraft is type approved
- A microlight aircraft is not permitted to overfly an assembly of persons or a congested area, town or settlement at any time, even at 1,500ft or above
- A microlight aircraft is not allowed to perform aerobatics at any time. Steep turns not exceeding 60 degrees angle of bank, intentional stalls from level flight including during a turn in level flight are not considered to be aerobatic manoeuvres
- A microlight aircraft is not permitted to fly at night.

PILOT'S MEDICAL

Before you can obtain a licence and can fly solo you must be in possession of a current Medical Certificate. When you have one it requires renewal dependent on your age:

Less than 40 years of age: 5 years
40 and over, but less than 50: 2 years
50 and over, but less than 70: 1 year
Over 70 years of age: 6 months

The cost of obtaining a medical certificate is levied by your doctor. There does not seem to be a set price: I have heard of fees ranging from £90.00 to nothing. The NPPL steering group has tried to get doctors to set a fee, but at the time of writing this has still not been set up.

PROPELLER

The propeller is no more than a revolving aerofoil generating 'lift', i.e. thrust, which either pulls or pushes an aircraft through the air. The illustration (*below*) shows how the angle of the propeller blade gets less from the root to the tip. Lift increases with both airspeed and angle of attack, so to ensure that the lift produced is uniform from root to tip for any given rate of revolution, the angle of the blade is higher at the root where the blade speed is lowest, and lower at the tip where the blade speed is highest.

There are two types of propeller arrangements: tractor and pusher. The tractor propeller pulls the aircraft through the air, while the pusher does what it says and pushes the aircraft through the air.

Each propeller arrangement has its advantages and disadvantages. The tractor propeller creates more lift from the 'slipstream' of the propeller over the inboard section of the wing, but the increased airflow it generates in front of

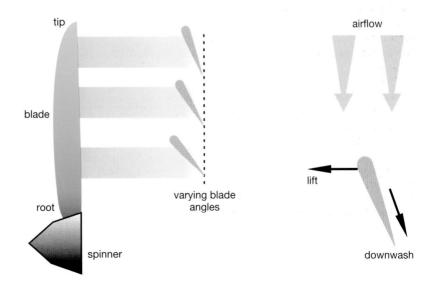

tip

blade

root

spinner

varying blade angles

airflow

lift

downwash

the aircraft means that open cockpit arrangements are more draughty. The pusher propeller is less draughty but less lift is obtained over the wing section, and the sensitivity of the rudder and elevator controls is increased.

Caring for the propeller is a chore that you must get used to. Apart from the fact they are very expensive, maximum efficiency demands a smooth-running and well-balanced propeller. The slightest imbalance can result in loose screws and a damaged engine. Small stones, mud and, more important, water will damage a revolving propeller – why?

Let us take as an example the direct-drive system, such as that on the Jabiru-powered Thruster T600N. Direct drive means that the propeller hub is directly attached to the crankshaft, so the propeller revolves at the same rate as the engine. If the engine is turning at 6,500rpm, the tips of the propeller – which in this case is 36in in diameter – will be rotating at 735mph – nearly supersonic. While the tips are rotating at such high speeds they are at their most brittle and can be damaged very easily.

To reduce tip speed a reduction gearbox can be fitted, though this does mean using a larger, 54in-diameter, propeller to generate sufficient thrust. If the same engine speed (6,500rpm) is geared down so the hub is now rotating at 2,600rpm, the tips of the propeller will now travel at approximately 420mph. At this kind of speed they can still be damaged, but they are not so brittle.

Contrary to popular belief, fitting a propeller on the aircraft the wrong way round will not make you go backwards. All that will be lost is a percentage of thrust, and your dignity.

PRESSURE

Air pressure is measured in millibars or hectopascals – the latter being the European word for millibars. There are two forms of pressure that pilots need to be aware of: static pressure and dynamic pressure.

Static Pressure

Static pressure is the barometric pressure, as recorded on a domestic barometer. In an aircraft, the altimeter measures barometric pressure and – because static pressure decreases at an even rate with altitude – registers it as a height.

QFE is the recorded pressure at airfield level. This is used while flying in close proximity of

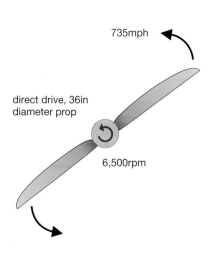

735mph

direct drive, 36in
diameter prop

6,500rpm

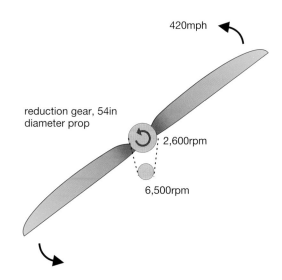

420mph

reduction gear, 54in
diameter prop

2,600rpm

6,500rpm

Reduction gearing for propellers.

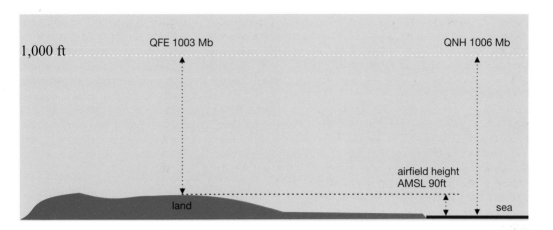

1,000 ft

QFE 1003 Mb

QNH 1006 Mb

airfield height
AMSL 90ft

land

sea

The difference between QFE and QNH.

the airfield or, what is more important, while in the circuit. The reading from this setting is referred to as height.

QNH is the recorded pressure at Average Mean Sea Level (AMSL). It is set on the altimeter when flying below 3,000ft away from the airfield and the reading from this setting is referred to as altitude. The UK is divided in Altimeter Setting Regions (ASRs) where the QNH is updated throughout the day, generally every hour.

Dynamic Pressure

Dynamic pressure is the measurement of moving air. Aircraft use this measurement to register their airspeed. The pitot tube always faces the airflow and as the aircraft moves through the airflow the airspeed indicator, which is linked to the pitot tube, measures the dynamic pressure in relation to the static pressure, the difference giving the airspeed.

During the Second World War a three-letter code – known as the Q code because each element began with the letter Q – was used to transmit radio signals between aircraft and air traffic control in Morse code. Some of these codes are still in use today, even though the reason particular letters were selected is no longer known – if there even was a reason in the first place. Here are a few you perhaps won't know:

QRA   The main station address
QRG   Exact frequency
QRK   Your readability
QRL   The frequency is in use
QRM   Man-made interference
QRN   Atmospheric noise
QRO   High power
QRP   Low power
QRQ   Please send faster
QRS   Please slow down
QRT   Close down
QRX   Please stand by
QRZ   Who is calling me?
QSA   Your signal strength
QSB   Fading
QSL   Confirmation of contact
QSO   A radio contact
QSY   Change frequency
QTH   The location you are transmitting from
QTR   What is exact time?

RADIATION FOG

Fog is basically strato cloud at low level. Fog is said to exist when the visibility falls below 1km, but in the UK the official figure is 180m before any public warnings are issued.

Radiation fog forms at night when the ground loses its heat and cools the air to saturation point. Fog forms near to the ground because the air near the surface falls below its dewpoint. Water vapour condenses and attaches onto dust and other particles, forming cloud at ground level which thickens overnight. It occurs when there are light winds and clear skies on long nights. Some fog will be burned off at dawn, and when the air eventually warms up it evaporates to produce tiny droplets of moisture.

There is a story that during the Second World War a squadron of Lancaster bombers was about to depart for a sortie to Germany. The first aircraft departed, the second aircraft was a bit slow in taxying; the conditions were ideal at that point – within five minutes the whole airfield was shrouded in fog, the first departing Lancaster having disturbed the air enough to form radiation fog.

Radiation fog.

RATINGS (ADDITIONS TO LICENCES)

A rating is an additional privilege attached to your licence. At the time of writing no privileges could be added to the NPPL, but I am sure this will change in the very near future. JAR licences and the old UK PPL can have the following ratings added:

- **IMC (Instrument Meteorological Conditions)**: allows the holder to fly out of VFR
- **Night Rating**: holder able to fly at night.

These of course only apply to SEP licences, the microlight licence is a VFR licence.

RIGHTS OF WAY

There are rights of way in the air as on the ground:

- Flying machines must give way to airships, gliders and balloons
- Airships must give way to gliders and balloons
- Gliders must give way to balloons
- An aircraft giving way must avoid passing over, under or crossing ahead of the other aircraft until well clear
- Aircraft on the ground must give way to those aircraft taking off or landing
- Aircraft on the ground must give way to any vehicle towing an aircraft
- Aircraft on the ground have right of way over vehicles

Radiation fog forming in a valley.

- When two aircraft are approaching to land, the lower aircraft has right of way
- An aircraft on final approach or landing has right of way over others in flight or on the ground
- If an aircraft is making an emergency landing, it has right of way over all other aircraft.

RIME ICE

This is a problem that shouldn't happen to a microlight aircraft, but it needs to be understood. It will arise if you inadvertently fly through cloud that has a relatively low moisture content and contains super-cooled water particles.

As these strike the aircraft they will freeze, creating icing in the form of an opaque white deposit normally confined to the leading edge of the wing and its immediate surrounding area. As it builds up, some may break away through the airflow, but enough can remain to disturb the airflow over the wing, so affecting lift and increasing the stall speed (*see* diagram, p.27).

Rime ice is usually found with stratiform cloud, where the super-cooled water particles are small.

ROTOR EFFECT

Low-level turbulence 'rotor' effects arise when it is windy, near an object such as a hill, range of hills, buildings, trees, and so on. Gentle light breezes are not really a problem as they just follow the contours of the object, flowing up the windward side and down the leeside, creating a sort of wave effect as shown in the illustration (*below*).

The problem starts when the wind increases in strength. Eddies form on the leeside: wild, moving air that can't be judged, is unpredictable, could force you down, and most certainly would give you a rough ride (*see* diagram, *bottom*).

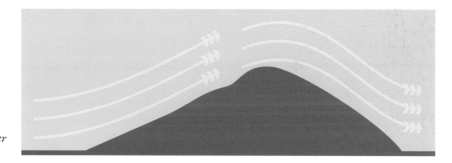

Light breeze over hills.

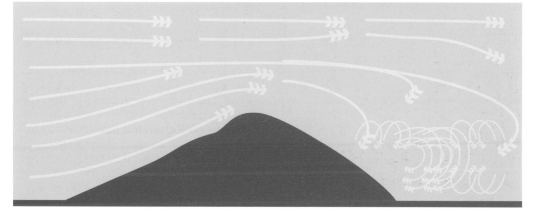

The same hill in a stronger breeze showing rotors on the leeside.

SALR (SATURATED ADIABATIC LAPSE RATE)

You will see from the illustration (*below*) that uneven heating will force air to rise at the dry adiabatic lapse rate until it reaches nearly the same temperature as the surrounding air. Then it will condense and continue rising until it reaches equilibrium at the saturated adiabatic lapse rate.

So, after condensation or the dewpoint level, latent heat is given off that effectively reduces the cooling rate of the air by half, at least up to 6,000ft. The cooling rate in the cloud is now rising at the SALR of 1.5°C per 1,000ft. The cloud this produces will be of the cumulus type, which can reach great heights before equilibrium is reached.

SEA BREEZE EFFECT

The air over the land heats quicker than the air over the sea, so the warm air over the land rises and the cooler air from the sea flows in to replace it – an onshore breeze. This is normally prevalent during the day. If conditions are suitable at night the reverse happens, creating an offshore breeze.

Height in feet	Air temp	Temp of Rising Air	Lapse Rates
6000	-2 Deg	2 Deg	
5000	0 Deg	3.5 Deg	S.A.L.R. Per 1,000 ft 1.5 Deg
4000	2 Deg	5.0 Deg	
3000	5 Deg	6.5 Deg	Dew point Condensation Starts
2000	8 Deg	9.5 Deg	D.A.L.R. Per 1,000 ft 3 Deg
1000	11 Deg	12.5 Deg	
Ground	15 Deg	15.5 Deg	

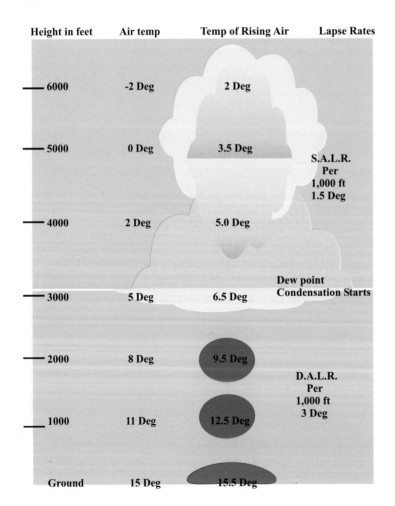

SALR (saturated adiabatic lapse rate).

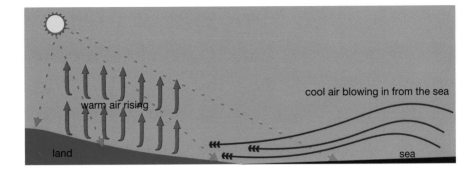

Sea breeze effect.

SPIRAL DIVE

The spiral dive is usually caused by an incorrect or badly coordinated steep turn. The bank angle is increased and the power is increased, but the pilot has neglected to input pitch (nose up). This results in a speedy turn with a massive loss of height in a short space of time, an increase in airspeed to dangerous levels if not corrected quickly, and also disorientation. The correct procedure for recovery from a spiral dive is as follows:

1. Power off, down to idle
2. Roll wings level
3. Ease – and I mean *ease*! – out of the dive until the airspeed returns to something like normal, then return to a safe mode of flight.

A safe mode of flight could mean climbing back up to a safe height, or resuming straight and level flight: it depends how much height you have lost.

STALLS

For any aerofoil to produce lift efficiently the flow of air over its surface must be smooth and unbroken ('laminar'). Air has the properties of a liquid, and tends to stick to the aerofoil section. However, there is a point at which it can break away: this is known as the stall and occurs when the aircraft's safe angle of attack has been exceeded. In the illustrations (*above right*) you will see three differing stages of an aerofoil; in illustration 'C', the smooth laminar flow has all but gone and with

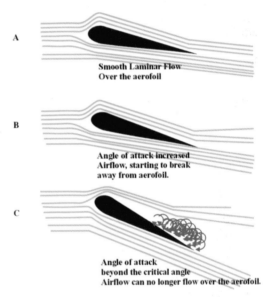

A

Smooth Laminar Flow
Over the aerofoil

B

Angle of attack increased
Airflow, starting to break
away from aerofoil.

C

Angle of attack
beyond the critical angle
Airflow can no longer flow over the aerofoil.

Stages in a stall.

it a reduction in the pressure that provides the major part of total lift.

High-Speed Stall

There is a saying in aviation 'airspeed is life, and altitude is life insurance'. But don't run away with the idea that a lack of airspeed combined with a high angle of attack is the only way an aerofoil can stall – there is also a condition known as a 'high-speed stall' or 'dynamic stall'.

Imagine you are in a dive, at a reasonably high airspeed and you consider the best course of action would be to pitch the nose up: the

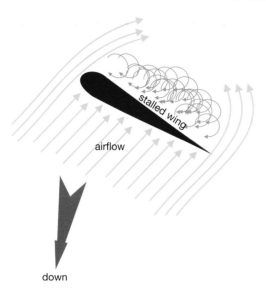

High-speed stall.

SUBLIMATION

This is the chemical process for turning water into ice crystals; *see* 'Rime Ice' and 'Ice'.

SWEEPBACK

Flex-wing (weight-shift) aircraft do not have a tailplane, so with these types of aircraft there is a marked degree of sweepback on the wings. The area in question is in the proximity of each wingtip; it acts as a fixed surface aft of the centre of gravity, and gives stability in pitch.

nose of the aircraft will almost certainly go up, but initially the aircraft will continue going down. If the stalling angle is exceeded then the smooth airflow over the wing will break away and the aerofoil will in fact stall, even though your airspeed is well above that of the stall speed of the aircraft.

You will see from the illustration (*above*), that in a dynamic or high-speed stall the air-flow immediately above the aerofoil is non-existent: all the aerofoil is doing is acting like a brake. The airflow goes either side of the aerofoil and the descent is fairly rapid, which is not so good close to the ground.

TAF

TAF stands for 'Terminal Aerodrome Fore-cast', and there is an adage with TAFs:

- If there is one line of text, it's flyable
- Two lines, it might be okay
- Three lines, forget it.

The Terminal Aerodrome Forecast is issued and reported to the Met Office, who provide it to be read by pilots, who then try to predict the weather. The TAF is broken down by codes as follows:

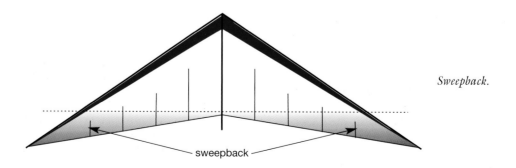

Sweepback.

- There is generally an ICAO code for the aerodrome the TAF is for, e.g. **EGSS** (Stanstead)
- The date and the time of the origin, e.g. **130500Z** (13th of the month, 0500hr Zulu, i.e. Greenwich Mean Time)
- The validity time, e.g. **130716** (0700 to 1600 on the 13th)
- The wind, e.g. **31015G25KT** (310 degrees @15kt, gusting to 25kt)
- The minimum visibility, e.g. **8000** (8km)
- The significant weather, e.g. -**SHRA** (light rain showers)
- The cloud, e.g. **FEW005 SCT010 SCT018CB BKN025** (few at 500ft, scattered at 1,000ft, scattered cumulonimbus at 1,800ft, broken at 2,500ft).
- The significant changes are represented by e.g. **PROB30** (30 per cent probability)
- The change indicator is formatted, e.g. **BECMG 1416** (becoming from 1400 to 1600), and **FM 1400TSRA BKN010CB** (from 1400 thunderstorm with rain, broken cumulonimbus at 1,000ft)

So TAF reading like this:

EGGY 300900,301019,23010KT,999,
SCT010,BKN018<BECMG
1114,6000,-RA,BKN012,TEMPO,1418,
2000,DZ,OVC004,FM1800,
30020G30KT,999,-SHRA,BKN015CB-

Would decode as follows:

- Luton, issued at 0900hr on the 30th, valid from 1000hr to 1900hr on the 30th
- Wind 230 degrees 10kt, 10km or more visibility, scattered cloud at 1,000ft, broken cloud at 1,800ft
- Becoming from 1100hr to 1400hr, visibility 6000m, slight rain, broken cloud at 1,200ft
- Temporarily 1400hr to 1800hr 2000m visibility, moderate drizzle, overcast cloud at 400ft
- From 1800hr wind 300 degrees at 20kt gusting to 30kt, 10km visibility, slight rain showers, cloud broken cumulonimbus (thunderstorm cloud) at 1,500ft, end

As I said before, the day described above wouldn't be a flyable day – three or more lines of text! Listed below are some of the most used codes written in TAFs:

BC	Patches
BL	Blowing
BR	Mist
DR	Drifting
DS	Dust storm
DU	Dust
DZ	Drizzle
FC	Funnel cloud
FG	Fog
FU	Smoke
FZ	Freezing
GR	Hail
GS	hail/snow
HZ	Haze
IC	Ice crystals
MI	Shallow
PL	Ice pellets
PO	Dust devils
PR	Banks
RA	Rain
SA	Sand
SH	Showers
SG	Snowgrain
SN	Snow
SQ	Squalls
SS	Sandstorm
TS	Thunder
VC	Vicinity

Cloud is defined as:

SKC	Sky clear	(0 oktas)
FEW	Few	(1–2 oktas)
SCT	Scattered	(3–4 oktas)
BKN	Broken	(5–7 oktas)
OVC	Overcast	

(oktas = eighths of cloud)

The two cloud types that are reported are TCU (towering cumulonimbus) and CB (cumulonimbus).

In the trend section, BECMG = becoming, TEMPO = temporarily, NOSIG = no significant change and NSW = no significant weather. *See also* METAR (Meteorological Aerodrome Report).

THUNDERSTORMS

Thunderstorms generally occur in fully developed cumulonimbus clouds. Large water droplets can form in the vigorous up-currents and freeze; they can be broken down by the up-currents, leading to them becoming positively electrified. The air becomes charged and eventually, when there is enough charge in the air, a lightning flash occurs.

We need three basic ingredients to make a thunderstorm. The basic fuel is moisture (water vapour) in the lowest levels of the atmosphere. The air above the lowest levels has to cool off rapidly with height, so that 2–3 miles above the ground it is very cold. Finally, we need something in the atmosphere to push that moist air from near the ground up to where the air around it is cold.

Thunder

The word 'thunder' is derived from Thor, the Norse god of thunder. He was supposed to be a red-bearded man of tremendous strength, his greatest attribute being the ability to forge thunderbolts. The word Thursday is also derived from his name.

Thunder is the sharp or rumbling sound that accompanies lightning. It is caused by the intense heating and expansion of the air along the path of the lightning. The rumble of thunder is caused by the noise passing through layers of the atmosphere at different temperatures. Thunder lasts longer than lightning because of the time it takes for the sound to travel from different parts of the flash.

How Far Away is the Thunderstorm?

This can be roughly estimated by measuring the interval between the lightning flash and the start of the thunder. If you count the time in seconds and then divide by three, you will have the approximate distance in kilometres. Thunder is rarely heard at a distance of more than 20km.

Thunderstorms can affect the microlighter in every sense, and the effects can be felt as far away as 30 miles. Close to a thunderstorm the updraughts and downdraughts are unpredictably strong, with windshear and gusts far in excess of what the aircraft is designed for, so: 'Black and grey, stay away!'

TROPOPAUSE/TROPOSPHERE

The weather only occurs within a narrow band of the atmosphere called the troposphere, within which it has a lapse rate set as the International Standard Atmosphere (ISA) lapse

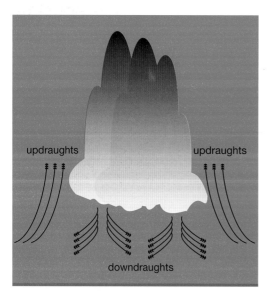

Effects of a thunderstorm.

Lightning in contact with the ground.

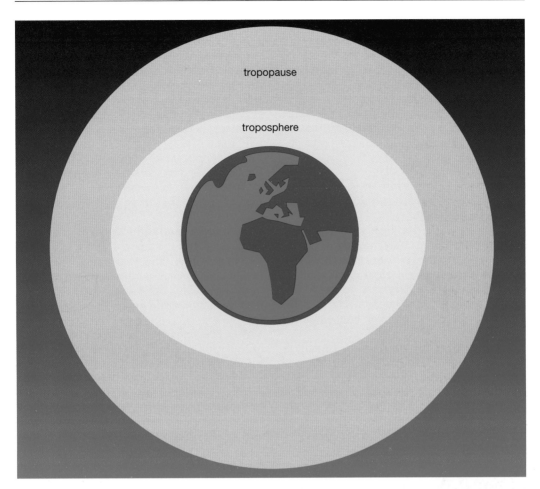

Tropopause and troposphere.

rate of 1.98°C per 1,000ft. This ISA lapse rate applies right up to the tropopause. Above the tropopause lies the stratosphere.

The troposphere's height above the surface of the earth varies depending where you are on the earth. At the poles it reaches up to approximately 30,000ft, and at the equator it reaches up to approximately 50,000ft.

TURNING IN BALANCE

A balanced turn during flight is one where the aircraft is turning at the correct bank angle, at a constant airspeed and with no skid or slip. There is an instrument fitted in most 3-axis

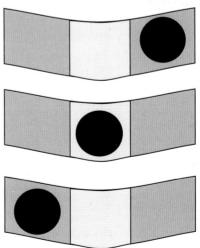

Balance ball.

machines to help you find out if you are making a balanced turn – the balance ball.

- Balance ball to the right: more right rudder needed, so 'stand on the ball' by pressing right rudder
- Balance ball in the middle: balance correct
- Balance ball to the left: more left rudder needed, so 'stand on the ball' by pressing left rudder.

So much for the 3-axis machines, but how can we tell if we are in balance during a turn in a weight-shift aircraft?

The airflow is a good indication as it hits you in the face: if you are turning to the left and feel the airflow on your right cheek then you are skidding to the right, if you feel the airflow on your left cheek then you are slipping to the left, and when you feel the airflow straight in your face then you are completing a balanced turn.

Some weight-shift pilots attach a small ribbon to the aerial on the front of the pod, which helps to recognize an unbalanced turn: if you are out of balance the ribbon will blow over to one side or the other.

TWO-STROKE CYCLE

Many microlight aircraft in use today are powered by the two-stroke engine, so a lot has to be said about the two-stroke. I believe it has its place in the market as an affordable method of obtaining an aircraft as they are in some cases considerably cheaper than their four-stroke cousins.

The downside of two-stroke engines is that they are sometimes unreliable, they certainly use more fuel, and the oil that you have to mix with the fuel is expensive. The reason they are less economical in operation than a four-stroke is that they work a lot harder.

The two-stroke engine has two cycles, hence 'two-stroke'; these are:

Compression and induction Fuel mixture is introduced into the top of the cylinder though the 'bypass inlet', and then compressed as the piston goes up; at the same time a new supply of fuel mixture is introduced through an inlet into the crankcase below.

Power and exhaust The compressed mixture in the cylinder is ignited by the spark plug at the end of the compression stroke, it expands and drives the piston back down the cylinder, providing power to the driveshaft. At the same time the exhaust outlet is exposed to allow the burnt gases to escape, and the bypass inlet is also exposed so that the down-going piston forces the new fuel mixture from the crankcase through the bypass into the top of the cylinder.

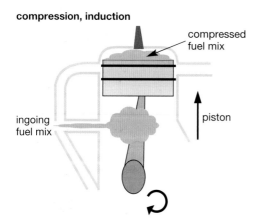

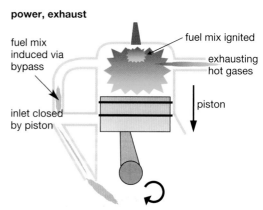

The two-stroke cycle.

ULTRALIGHT

American for microlight – enough said!

UNDERCARRIAGE

Many pilots tend to forget about the undercarriage of the aircraft, because it doesn't affect normal flight. However, during the take-off and landing phases of flight the undercarriage becomes quite an important factor.

Little nicks and cuts in the tyre wall may not look a problem, but there could be underlying damage, so tyres should be checked as thoroughly as the fuel. Correct pressures is something that quite often escapes the notice of the pilot: some do check, but most wait for the tyre to go down before going to the car, getting the foot-pump and re-inflating the tyre, without a thought as to why it went flat in the first place.

Heavy landings should be reported and the aircraft thoroughly checked before any further flights are undertaken. If you have a heavy landing and the result is a flat tyre, that means that most of the impact was absorbed by the tyre. On the other hand, if after the same heavy landing your tyres are okay, then where did all the shock go? One possible answer is that it went throughout the airframe of the aircraft, so it's a good idea to get the aircraft checked after a heavy arrival.

VALLEY WINDS

Valley winds move uphill during the day (anabatic) and downhill at night (katabatic). They are caused by solar heating expanding the air along a slope; this air is forced outwards and upwards by the cold air lying above, which is heaviest in the valley since there is a thicker layer.

As this process continues, cool air sinking in the middle of the valley is heated, and a general circulation is set up. This generally happens in the morning; it reaches its maximum by the noon/early afternoon.

At early evening, just before the sun sets, the sun's heat is diminishing, the ground cools and the air above it cools. This cooler air, being heavier than the surrounding air, seeks the lower level, therefore it flows down the slope to the centre of the valley.

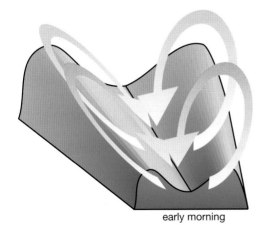

early morning

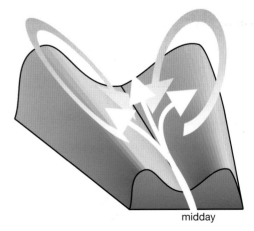

midday

Anabatic (left) *and katabatic* (right) *winds.*

Imagine this happening in a Scottish or Welsh mountain valley. As the night goes by, the air close to the ground gets colder and colder, and often ends up as a large pool of cold, dense air. This can then spill over the side of the mountain where gravity takes over. This cold wind drains down the mountainside to the valley below as a cold katabatic wind. In the UK these katabatic winds are generally quite light, in the order of 5–10mph (8–16km/h), but in other places around the world they can be very much stronger.

The most famous katabatic wind in Europe is the Mistral, which blows down the Rhône Valley in southern France and out into the Mediterranean. It can be very strong, reaching speeds of 80mph as it funnels down over the Rhône delta, and is generally at its strongest in winter and early spring.

VELOCITY

There are several velocities that the pilot of any aeroplane must know, in the interests of safe aircraft handling. They differ according to aeroplane type, and the three most significant are:

- **VNE (Velocity Never Exceed)** This airspeed is usually below the airspeed at which the aircraft will break up in the air.

- **VA** This is the maximum manoeuvring airspeed of an aircraft, when turbulent conditions are evident. Usually the VA is twice that of the stall speed VS (below).

- **VS** This is the stall speed of the aircraft.

VNE, VA and VS are all listed in the aircraft's pilot's operating manual and should be placarded in the cockpit of the aircraft.

VERTICAL SPEED INDICATOR (VSI)

The VSI indicates the rate at which an aircraft is climbing or descending, in feet per minute. There is an aperture in the VSI for instant exit/entry for static pressure, allowing the static pressure to inflate or deflate a set of bellows. There is also a pinhole in the case for the gradual exit/entry of static pressure, which allows the air around the bellows to be affected by the static pressure.

In level flight the static pressure both inside the bellows and around the outside of the bellows is the same, and the instrument will register no climb or descent.

During a climb the pressure in the bellows decreases as air instantly exits into the lower atmospheric pressure outside. Pressure on the bellows is now temporarily greater due to the pinhole aperture allowing a gradual exit of air around it into the atmosphere, and the instrument will register the rate of climb.

During a descent, the pressure in the bellows increases as air instantly enters the bellows from the higher atmospheric pressure outside. Pressure on the bellows is now temporarily less due to the pinhole aperture allowing only a gradual entry of air into the casing, causing the instrument to register the rate of descent.

Remember that pressure decreases the higher you go and increases the lower you go. The VSI has a bit of a delay, so that after you have levelled off after a climb or a descent the instrument may show some rate of descent or climb for a while afterwards. So don't 'chase' the VSI, check the altimeter.

VFR AND VMC

VFR (Visual Flight Rules) appertaining to microlight pilots are as follows:

- Always be clear of cloud and in sight of the surface
- Always have an in-flight visibility of not less than 3km
- When above 3,000ft AMSL: have an in-flight visibility of not less than 5km; never be less than 1500m from cloud horizontally; and never be less than 1,000ft from cloud vertically.

This applies to all airspace other than controlled airspace, and up to an altitude of 10,000ft.

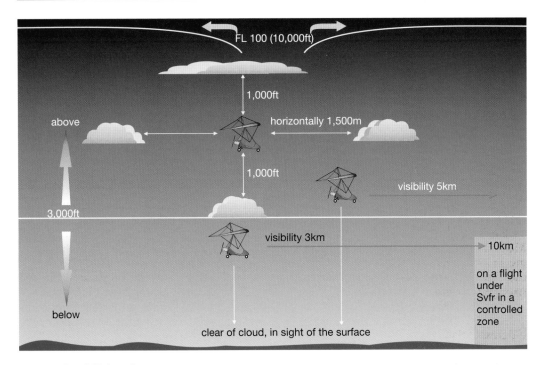

FL 100 (10,000ft)

1,000ft

above

horizontally 1,500m

1,000ft

visibility 5km

3,000ft

visibility 3km

10km

on a flight under Svfr in a controlled zone

below

clear of cloud, in sight of the surface

ABOVE: *Visual flight rules.*

Washout.

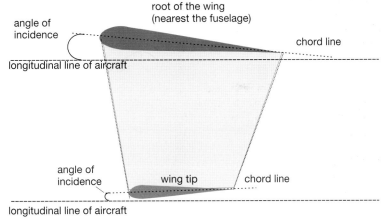

root of the wing
(nearest the fuselage)

angle of incidence

chord line

longitudinal line of aircraft

angle of incidence

wing tip

chord line

longitudinal line of aircraft

The diagram (*top*) illustrates VMC (Visual Meteorological Conditions).

You need 10km visibility to accept a Special Visual Flight Rules (SVFR) flight in controlled airspace. An SVFR flight is one where the pilot is given permission to penetrate controlled airspace when the necessary qualifications to do so are not held. In all cases SVFR flights can only be made with clearance from Air Traffic Control (ATC).

WASHOUT

Washout is a design feature of weight-shift aircraft, shown in the illustration above. The angle of incidence (the built-in angle of attack

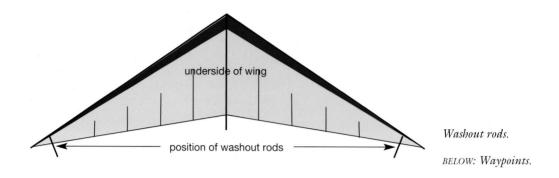

underside of wing

position of washout rods

Washout rods.

BELOW: *Waypoints.*

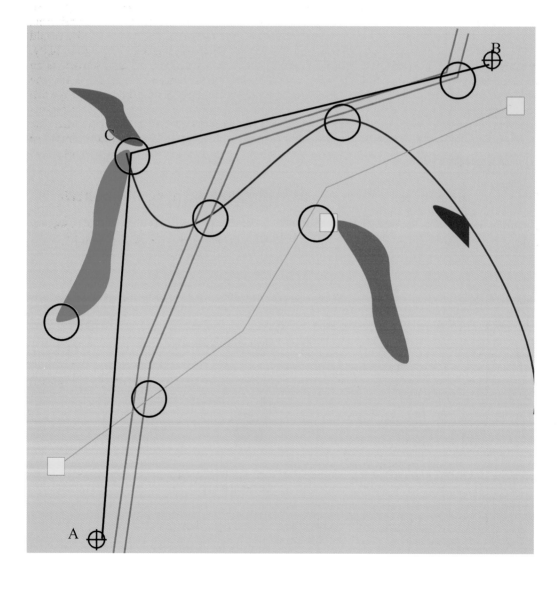

of the wing, in relation to the datum line on the aircraft) is greater at the root than at the tips of the wing – I have exaggerated the angle for the purposes of the drawing. Therefore, as a high angle of attack begins to bring on the stall, the inboard parts of the wing stall first, leaving the tips still flying.

WASHOUT RODS

Sometimes the washout rods on weight-shift aircraft cause confusion, because of their name. They have nothing to do with washout, instead their name derives from their being at the washout end of the wing.

Washout rods allow the wingtips to assume whatever angle is dictated by the airflow at lower speeds, but come into play as minimum washout stops when the wing is dived and therefore plays a part in dive limitation and recovery.

WAYPOINTS

Waypoints are easily recognizable features marked on a chart along an intended route to be flown; they can be on that track or to one side of the track line. When sighted, waypoints confirm your position, your timing and that you are heading in the right direction. You will see from the diagram (*opposite page, bottom*) that the route (trackline) is from A to B via C; there are a series of circles en route that mark prominent features either on track or just to the side of it. Natural features are always a good guide as these don't often move, or else you can use things such as junctions in major roads.

WEIGHT AND BALANCE

This is mainly applicable to 3-axis types. An overloaded aircraft may fail to become airborne, while an out-of-limits centre of gravity would seriously affect the controllability and stability.

All 3-axis types have what is known as an 'envelope': stay within this envelope and the aircraft should perform as the manual says. Go beyond the envelope and serious implications to the stability of the aircraft could ensue. The diagram (*below*) is a hypothetical example of what a centre of gravity envelope looks like.

WINDSHEAR/WIND GRADIENTS

Windshear is a change in both direction and/or the wind speed; *see* 'Gradients (Wind)'.

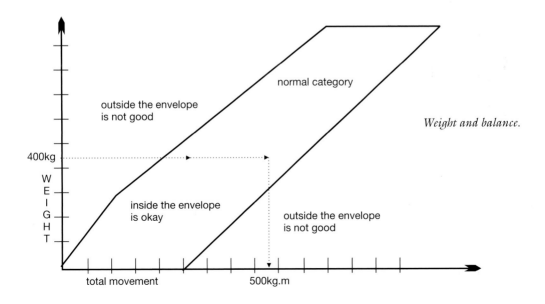

Weight and balance.

X RATING

I thought long and hard about the letter 'X' and all I could come up with is the 'X' Rating, which is an examiner rating for microlight instructors. The instructor who has an 'X' rating can test you for your General Flying Test (GFT).

Should you want to become an instructor on microlight aircraft, then of course the first step is a microlight licence. At the time of writing there is no route to attach an instructor rating to the new NPPL (M), but the NPPL steering group are negotiating hard with the CAA to correct that.

Instructor (Microlight)

To become an instructor on microlight aircraft you must meet the following criteria:

- Held a PPL for at least eight months
- Completed at least 100 hours P1 (if you hold a SEP licence, be it JAR or NPPL, then you can credit some of those P1 hours to the cause)
- Have a willingness to impart information.

Enrolment on an AFI (Assistant Flying Instructor) course is the next step, this being with a FIC (Flying Instructor Course) instructor – these are normally FIEs (Flying Instructor Examiners). The course normally takes about three weeks' full time and is quite intensive, with forty hours of groundschool and fifteen hours of flying tuition. It usually starts with a 'mini GFT', to see if you are a good flyer, then an entrance exam; if this sounds off-putting don't worry – it's not all that bad!

Once you have completed your course, and taken and passed an initial AFI test, you are let loose on your unsuspecting students for a minimum of thirteen months and a minimum of 100 instructional hours under the guidance of a QFI (Qualified Flying Instructor). Once this is completed and your upgrade test has been passed you are a QFI yourself. A rewarding and satisfying job that doesn't pay all that well, unless we have perfect weather and loads of students!

YAW

Yaw happens when the aeroplane slips inwards or skids outwards away from its intended direction of travel. The rudder is often mistakenly thought of as being the correct means of achieving a turn in an aeroplane, but turns with directional stability are accomplished with the use of rudder and aileron. Think of steering a car on an icy road: you might turn the wheel, and the tyres may turn in the direction of the steering wheel, but the car may go straight on. Imagine now an aeroplane constantly on ice, in other words with nothing to grip: an input of rudder alone will result in a skid along its path, at least for a short while.

The further effect of yaw is that it can induce a roll. An input of rudder will have the aeroplane skidding outwards, but as the aeroplane moves around its vertical axis the inner wing will move slower than the outer wing. The faster wing will of course produce more lift and so rise, while the slower or inner wing will decrease its lift and drop, as shown in the diagram (*opposite page, top*).

Yaw can also be a product of aileron input: when the down-going aileron increases the angle of attack on the outer wing, it creates an increase in induced drag that causes the aircraft to yaw in the opposite way to the intended turn. This is known as adverse yaw. Adverse yaw is countered by the use of rudder, and can be eased by the fitting of differential ailerons.

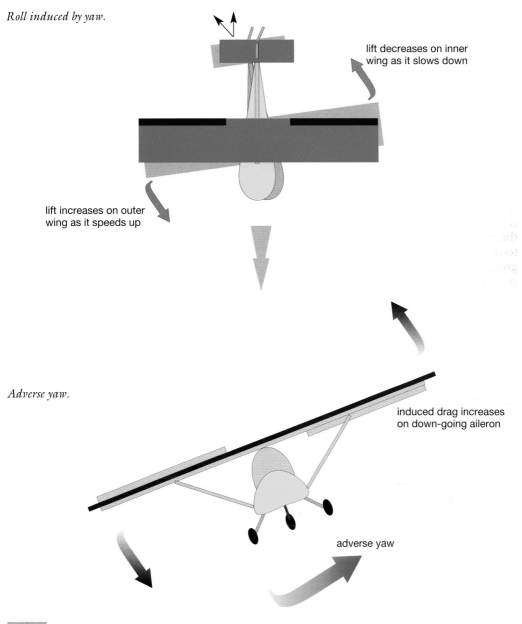

Roll induced by yaw.

lift decreases on inner
wing as it slows down

lift increases on outer
wing as it speeds up

Adverse yaw.

induced drag increases
on down-going aileron

adverse yaw

ZONES

This term is loosely used to mean the circuit, circuit patterns and flying in and around ATZs.

All circuits are left-hand by default, unless otherwise stated. This means that if you are flying in the vicinity of an aerodrome all turns are to the left, this includes descending turns, and certainly while in the circuit.

You will at some point in your flying career leave the comfort of your home airfield and depart on a flight somewhere else. The usual way to depart the circuit is as shown in the

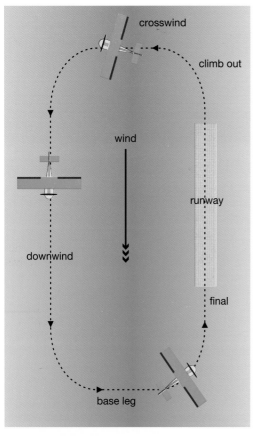

crosswind

climb out

wind

runway

downwind

final

base leg

diagram (*opposite page, top*), unless local rules differ. If departing in any of the ways shown, please continue climbing!

When you come back to your home airfield, or indeed when you arrive at your destination airfield, you will have to join the circuit.

Before joining any ATZ or aerodrome overhead, make sure you have PPR-d, or contacted them by radio and obtained joining information. You should have set the QFE for that airfield on your altimeter so that when you join the circuit you will be at the same height above ground level as all the other aircraft in the pattern at that time. This is important as the separation is then non-existent: you will be able to see the other aircraft simply as they are the same height (AGL) as you. There is a simple check that you can perform every time you intend to land at an alien airfield.

- Set correct QFE
- Know whether it is a left- or right-hand circuit pattern – simple if you PPR before you set out

Standard circuit.

BELOW: *Graphical circuit.*

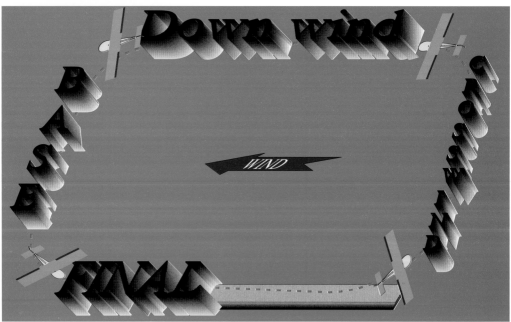

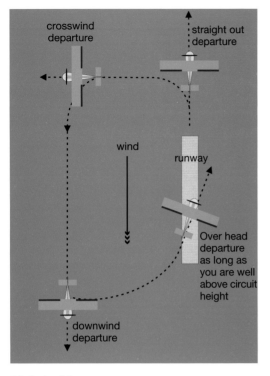

Methods of departure.

- Avoid sensitive areas, avoid upsetting the neighbours
- Know about wake turbulence separation
- If using the radio keep the calls brief and unambiguous; if non-radio, know your light signals
- If you have to go-around make sure you move to the dead-side, so that you are flying parallel to the runway
- Don't be shy about asking for directions when on the ground, if you are unsure of where to go
- Remember to taxi clear of the active runway
- Never cross an active runway without permission; you may have landed into wind on a non-active runway because the controller was feeling kind, but the active runway may be a crosswind one
- When you have parked up and made your aircraft secure make your way to the building with the big black 'C' on a yellow background, sign in and pay your landing fee
- Aerodromes are dangerous places, even small friendly microlight clubs, be aware at all times for yourself and others.

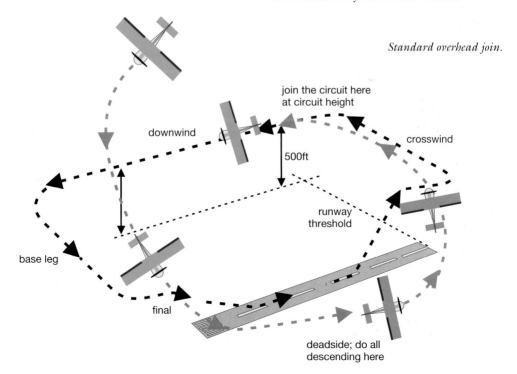

Standard overhead join.

The Syllabus for the NPPL(M) 3-Axis and Weight-Shift Aircraft

The syllabus for microlight training in the UK has been formulated by consulting experienced microlight instructors and examiners. The microlight panel of examiners on behalf of the BMAA, must be accredited with the contents and structure of the syllabus, and its approval by the CAA. I have adhered to the structure of the syllabus, and added a few of my own anecdotes and tips. This manual must be used in conjunction with the official BMAA-approved syllabus, and of course with a qualified instructor.

NB: This is not intended as a 'teach-yourself' manual. All the exercises in the following pages should be carried out under the supervision of a qualified microlight instructor.

The 3-Axis Microlight NPPL(M) Syllabus

Exercise 1. Aircraft Familiarization

Exercise 2. Preparation for Flight and Action After

Exercise 3. Air Experience

Exercise 4. Effects of Controls

Exercise 5. Taxying

Exercise 6. Straight and Level

Exercise 7. Climbing

Exercise 8. Descending

Exercise 9a. Medium-Level Turns (up to 30 Degrees of Bank)

Exercise 9b. Climbing and Descending Turns

Exercise 10a. Slow Flight

Exercise 10b. Stalling

Exercise 11. Spin Awareness

Exercise 12. Take-Off and Climb to Downwind

Exercise 13. The Circuit, Approach and Landing/Overshoot

Exercise 14. Advanced Turns (up to and including 60 Degrees of Bank)

Exercise 15. Unusual Attitudes

Exercise 16a. Forced Landings, with/without Power

Exercise 16b. Operation at Minimum Level

Exercise 17a. First Solo

Exercise 17b. Solo Circuit, General Flying

Exercise 17c. Dual Revision for GFT

Exercise 18. Navigation

The syllabus for a full NPPL(M) licence requires a minimum instructional period of twenty-five hours. Ten of these hours must be solo and must include five hours' navigation training, where two solo cross-country flights are completed. A restricted licence requires a minimum instructional period of fifteen hours, of which seven must be solo.

Exercises 1, 2 and 3

These first exercises are usually taken as an air-experience flight, and consist of you – the student – taking to the air with an instructor at the school of your choice.

Exercise 1 is aircraft familiarization, finding out the different parts that make up the aircraft and where you will sit while flying, and being given a general brief on safety aspects.

Exercise 2 is preparing the aircraft for flight, refuelling if necessary, pre-flight checks, and learning where you will be flying and at what heights.

Exercise 3 is the actual air-experience flight, your chance to fly the aircraft and experience the feeling of flying. Generally these flights are of twenty to sixty minutes' duration.

Many flying clubs arrange air-experience flights, so you can have a go before committing yourself to a course of flying lessons.

Exercise 4

THE EFFECTS OF CONTROLS

The aim of this exercise is to understand how each control affects the aircraft during flight. Exercise 4 is the basis of all your flying training: learning anything new starts with the foundation, so get to grips with this exercise and the rest of your training will follow easily.

Your instructor should at this point have told you how each flight during your training will be handled and, what is more important, how control is handed over between you and him. Generally the conversation goes like this: (instructor) 'You have control'; (student) 'I have control', and vice versa.

Exercise 4 looks at how the controls move different moveable surfaces on the aircraft during flight and how moving these surfaces makes the aircraft turn, descend and climb. Each control has a primary effect and a secondary effect.

Your instructor will demonstrate each control in turn with you 'following through' to feel the effect that each control has. He will then guide you through having a go yourself with and without his verbal help. The main controls are:

- Elevators, which are located on the rear of the aircraft on the tailplane and which control pitch
- Ailerons, which are located on each wing and control roll
- Rudder, which is located on the rear of the aircraft on the trailing edge of the fin and controls yaw
- Throttle, which makes the engine turn faster or slower
- Trim, which eases the forces on certain controls, to make piloting easier.

The 3-axis aircraft has three planes of movement:

- Pitch, longitudinal movement about the lateral axis
- Roll, lateral movement about the longitudinal axis
- Yaw, longitudinal movement about the vertical axis (*see* diagram, p.8).

The pilot controls the motion of the aircraft around the three planes of movement with the main flight controls.

The effects of each control.

Control	Primary Effect	Further Effect
Elevator	Pitch	Airspeed change
Aileron	Roll	Yaw/Adverse yaw
Rudder	Yaw	Roll

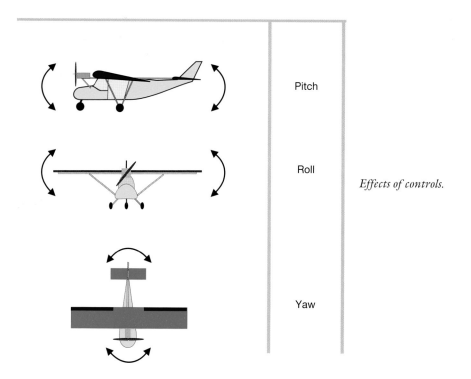

Pitch

Roll

Effects of controls.

Yaw

The illustration above explains what each control does to the aircraft in the air; let's look in a little more depth at each control.

THE ELEVATOR CONTROLS PITCH

The further effect of the elevator is an airspeed change: raising the nose with the elevator increases the angle of attack, which in turn increases drag and then reduces airspeed. Conversely, lowering the nose with the elevator will decrease the angle of attack, reduce the drag and then increase airspeed.

THE AILERONS CONTROL ROLL

Roll causes yaw – this is the secondary effect of ailerons. Once banked, the aircraft will slip

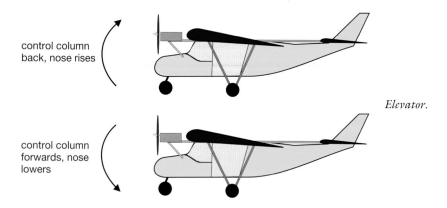

control column back, nose rises

control column forwards, nose lowers

Elevator.

towards the lower wing and yaw the aircraft in the direction of the slip. This will cause the aircraft to turn, and the nose to lower.

IMPORTANT: the aircraft will continue to roll until the control column is centralized.

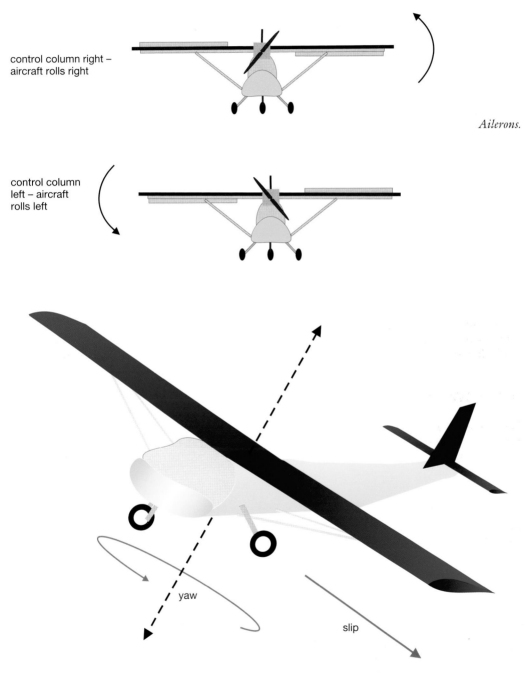

control column right –
aircraft rolls right

Ailerons.

control column left – aircraft rolls left

yaw

slip

Three-axis yawslip.

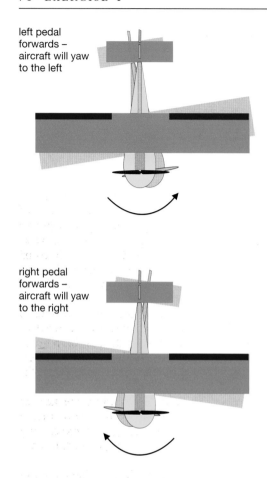

left pedal forwards – aircraft will yaw to the left

right pedal forwards – aircraft will yaw to the right

THE RUDDER CONTROLS YAW

The primary function of the rudder is to balance flight, to prevent yaw, as indicated by the balance ball:

- Ball central – no yaw
- Ball right – left yaw
- Ball left – right yaw.

Yaw causes roll – this is the secondary effect of rudder. As the aircraft yaws, the outside wing is travelling faster than the inside wing, and so generates more lift, inducing a roll into the yaw.

THE EFFECT OF POWER (THROTTLE)

An Increase of Power

1. The aircraft will accelerate, although this is temporary
2. The nose of the aircraft will rise to a new attitude and the aircraft will start to climb
3. The aircraft will settle to a new airspeed close to that of the original trimmed airspeed, though now climbing.

A Decrease of Power

1. The aircraft will decelerate, although this is temporary
2. The nose of the aircraft will lower to a new attitude and the aircraft will descend
3. The airspeed will settle to a new airspeed close to that of the original trimmed airspeed, though now descending.

The Effect of Slipstream and Airspeed

The higher the power, the more slipstream there is, so the more effective the rudder and the elevator will be. However, there is a tendency for the aircraft to yaw due to the corkscrew flow of air from the propeller striking the side of the fin.

At higher airspeeds the controls have a firmer feel and are more effective. At lower airspeeds the controls have a lighter feel and are less effective.

TRIM

The pitch control may be fitted with a trim system – most microlights today have this. The trim system adjusts the hands-off position in pitch and therefore in airspeed. Trim is controlled by selecting the desired attitude by use of the primary flying controls, then adjusting the trimmer until no pressure is needed on the control column to maintain that attitude.

Exercise 5

TAXYING

The aim of this exercise is to safely control the aircraft while manoeuvring on the ground in a variety of wind conditions and on different surfaces. There aren't many instructors who will devote a whole specific lesson to taxying: we teach you the correct way to taxi the aircraft from your first lesson, and then experience is built up over the remainder of your flying course, until this exercise is totally ingrained.

To start taxying the aircraft, we need to increase power – too much and the aircraft

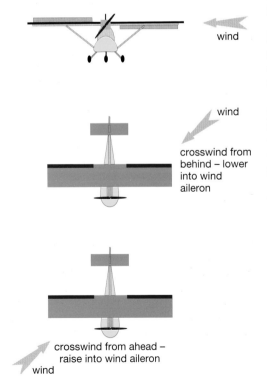

Crosswind taxying.

wind

crosswind from behind – lower into wind aileron

crosswind from ahead – raise into wind aileron
wind

will spring away, not enough and the aircraft won't move. The aircraft needs a surge of power to start taxying, then a gentler power setting to keep taxying. A sensible fast walking pace is fast enough and safe enough to taxi any aircraft; in an area where many other aircraft are parked, the taxi speed should be somewhat less.

Power should be reduced in good time to slow down, then the brakes used if needed. Microlight brakes have in the past been notoriously bad, and though they are getting better they should never be relied upon solely for stopping.

The ground surface should be checked for loose stones and other such hazards before applying large power settings to avoid causing damage to other aircraft and, indeed, to your own.

Steering the aircraft while taxying is accomplished by using the rudder pedals: push the right pedal to turn right, push the left pedal to turn left. Correct use of the controls while taxying can avoid embarrassing and expensive repairs.

While taxying you should position the controls to protect the aircraft as follows:

- **In a head wind** hold the control column neutral or back to ease the weight on the nosewheel.

- **In a tail wind** hold the control column neutral or forward to stop the wind from lifting the tailplane upward from behind.

- **In a crosswind from ahead** the wind is trying to lift the into-wind wing, so raise the into-wind aileron by moving the control column toward the wind.

- **In a crosswind from behind** the wind is trying to lift the into-wind wing, so lower the into-wind aileron by moving the control column away from the wind.

Also while taxying you must remember to:

- Check that the compass is working; as you turn right it should be decreasing and as you turn left it should be increasing

- Check that the slip ball moves whenever you turn the aircraft
- Monitor engine temperature and pressures – most aircraft engines are air cooled so while running for long periods on the ground they do tend to overheat
- Be aware of what is around you: other aircraft, people, etc.

Exercise 6

STRAIGHT AND LEVEL

The aim of this exercise is to attain and maintain flight in a straight line at a constant altitude, and also to do this at different airspeeds.

STRAIGHT FLIGHT

Keep the wings level with the horizon, using the ailerons. Keep the aircraft in balance using the rudder.

The saying is 'kick the ball', in other words kick the ball on the slip indicator:

- If the ball is to the left of centre, push the left rudder pedal to centre it
- If the ball is to the right of centre, push the right rudder to centre it.

Remember the secondary effects of control: rudder input leads to roll and aileron input leads

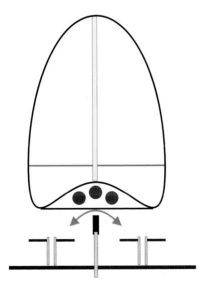

Straight and level flight.

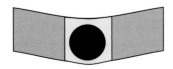

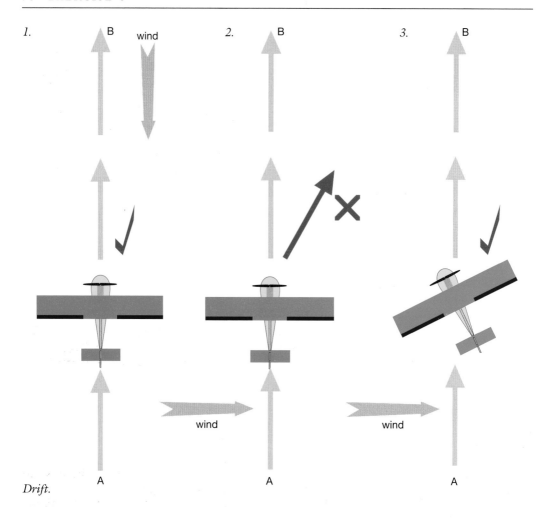

Drift.

to yaw, so keep the wings level with ailerons as you input the rudder, and be *gentle*.

DRIFT

While flying in a straight line a crosswind component will cause drift, so a drift angle has to be set up using a crosswind reference point: keep that reference point on a steady relative bearing.

You will see from the illustration above that if there is a headwind (1), no drift angle needs to be set up. If the wind is from the left (2), and if no drift angle is set up, the aircraft will move off track. When the correct drift angle is set up (3), the aircraft will maintain its origi-

nal track, although it will have a different heading.

BASIC CONTROL THEORY

HEIGHT is controlled by power, i.e. by the throttle.

AIRSPEED is controlled by pitch/attitude, i.e. by the elevator.

- **If the aircraft is descending** check that the aircraft is in trim and that the airspeed is

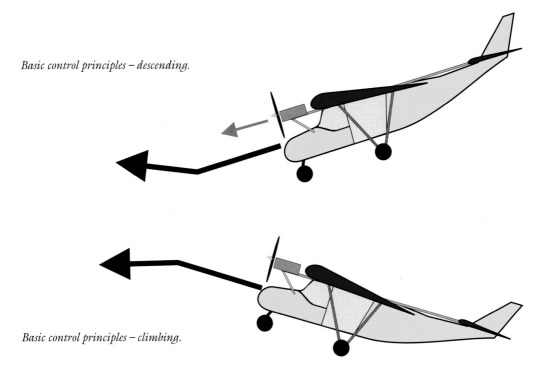

Basic control principles – descending.

Basic control principles – climbing.

correct. If you are still descending, increase the power and raise the nose.

- **If the aircraft is climbing** check that the aircraft is in trim and the airspeed is correct. If you are still climbing lower the nose and reduce the power.

TO CHANGE YOUR AIRSPEED IN LEVEL FLIGHT

Increasing Airspeed

P Power – increase power
A Attitude – change the attitude, lower the nose to maintain level flight
T Trim – use the trim to ease the pressure off the control column

Reducing Airspeed

P Reduce power
A Change the attitude, raise the nose to maintain level flight
T Use the trim to ease the pressure off the control column

The mnemonic PAT, and variations of it, will crop up many more times in the syllabus so you should remember them until they become ingrained.

In steady constant flight, nose attitudes will be higher for low airspeeds and lower for faster airspeeds.

Exercise 6 is one of the most demanding exercises for an instructor to teach and for a student to absorb. The exercise is a combination of coordination, awareness and hard work that arrives very early in the training syllabus; but master it, along with Exercises 4 and 5, and the basis of your training will be deep-rooted.

Exercise 7

CLIMBING

The aim of this exercise is to enter and maintain a steady full-power climb, in a straight line, and then to return to level flight at a predetermined altitude. This is the basis for all climbs, be they full-power, cruise or best rate climbs. Full-power climbs, obviously, are climbs using full engine power, and are usually used for take-off and other circumstances where maximum rate of climb for a given flight attitude is needed. Cruise climbs are climbs with no loss in airspeed but a slight decrease in engine power, usually used to keep the engine from over-heating. Best rate climbs are climbs that use the full power of the aircraft and as much pitch input as is possible.

THE FORCES INVOLVED

More power is needed in a climb to balance the increase in drag from the weight.

Drag also varies with airspeed, so climbing performance will also vary with airspeed.

To enter a climb, we need to do three things:

P Power – apply power, while balancing the aircraft with rudder

A Attitude – raise the nose to the climb attitude, then hold it

T Trim – adjust the attitude to achieve the correct airspeed, then trim for that desired airspeed

So, PAT again! During the climb maintain a good lookout and monitor the engine temperatures and pressures.

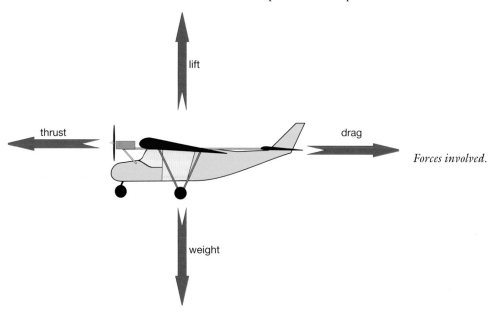

Forces involved.

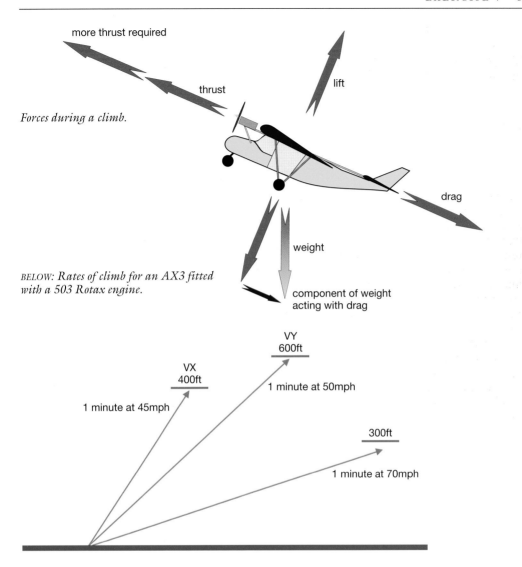

Forces during a climb.

BELOW: *Rates of climb for an AX3 fitted with a 503 Rotax engine.*

To level off after a climb when your desired altitude is attained:

A Lower the nose to level the attitude and maintain (or temporarily increase) your airspeed

P Reduce the power back to cruise RPM, while maintaining balance with the rudder

T Adjust the attitude to achieve the correct airspeed and power setting in order to maintain your chosen height, then trim to your desired airspeed

So this time it is ATP – attitude, power, trim.

Exercise 7 is normally completed along with Exercise 8, Descending, because what goes up must come down – it would seem silly just going up in the air and climbing all the while, so most instructors combine the two exercises.

Remember during this exercise to monitor the engine temperatures and pressures frequently as the engine is working hard; and maintain a really good lookout! Also remember that microlights must remain in sight of the surface at all times, and must keep clear of cloud.

Exercise 8

DESCENDING

The aim of this exercise is to enter and maintain a steady glide descent in a straight line, then at a predetermined altitude to return to level flight or enter a climb. Also to enter and maintain a steady cruise descent in a straight line.

THE FORCES

During a glide descent (i.e. with the engine throttled right back), a component of weight adds to the thrust or even takes its place. You will also find that with differing airspeeds, your descent rates can be altered. Remember during a glide descent that the engine can cool off quite quickly, so perform engine warms every 200–300ft.

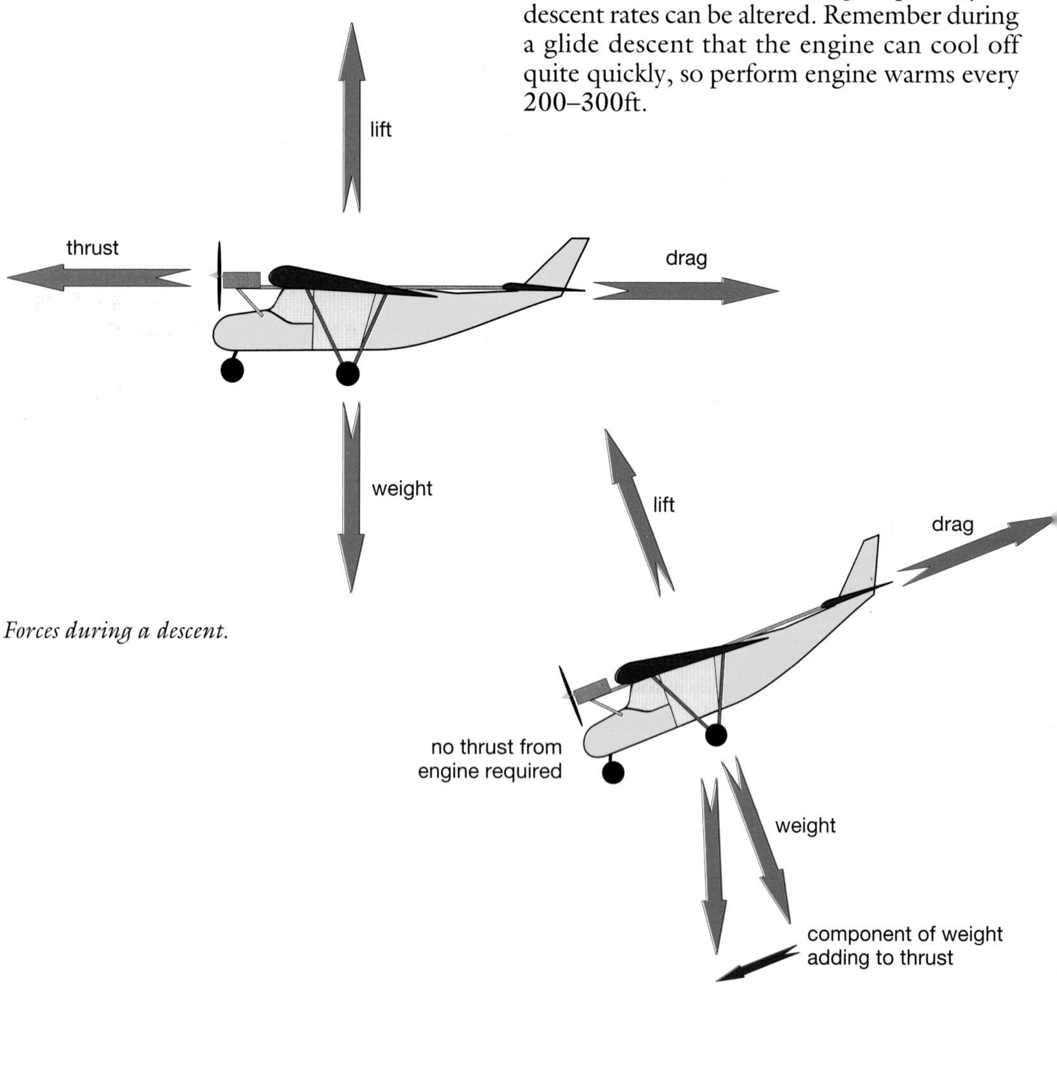

lift

thrust

drag

weight

Forces during a descent.

lift

drag

no thrust from engine required

weight

component of weight adding to thrust

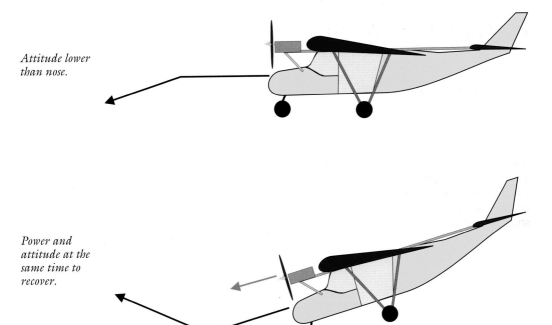

Attitude lower than nose.

Power and attitude at the same time to recover.

During a cruise descent (a descent using attitude and power), the power will reduce the angle and the rate of descent. However, a cruise descent helps the engine to keep warm during long descents, a factor to consider during carburettor icing conditions.

Entering the descent – APT

A Lower the nose to descent attitude (which will increase the airspeed)
P Reduce power as required, use the rudder to keep balance
T Adjust to achieve a desired airspeed

TO LEVEL OUT OR ENTER A CLIMB FROM A DESCENT – (P&A) T

(P&A) Apply power and change the attitude together (attitude slightly first if close to the ground)
T Adjust attitude to achieve a desired airspeed

Exercise 9a

MEDIUM-LEVEL TURNS

The aim of this exercise is to enter and maintain a medium-level turn (up to 30 degrees of bank) while maintaining level flight, then to return to straight and level flight on a new heading.

THE FORCES DURING THE TURN

During a 30-degree bank turn more lift is required to maintain level flight: due to the bank, some of the lift is no longer counter-acting weight, so without an increase in lift the aircraft will slip into the turn and descend. More lift can be produced by increasing the angle of attack, though this will reduce the

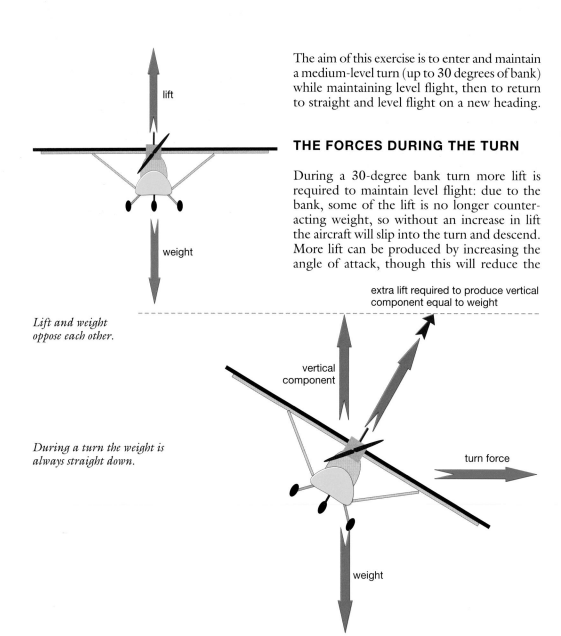

Lift and weight oppose each other.

During a turn the weight is always straight down.

airspeed, by approximately 5mph. Power can be used if necessary to maintain airspeed.

TO MAINTAIN THE TURN

Monitor the bank angle by using the horizon in relation to the aircraft structure – where the jury struts meet the wing, for instance; if your aircraft has a vertical bar in the screen, use that to judge 30 degrees and use something on that strut to maintain your pitch input.

- Keep the aircraft in balance using the rudder during the turn
- Monitor the height using a visual reference on the aircraft or by using the VSI and the altimeter
- Monitor the airspeed – if it drops below acceptable margins, increase the RPM and relax a little back pressure on the control column (acceptable margins are a loss of approximately 5mph airspeed in relation to normal cruising airspeed, during a 30-degree turn).

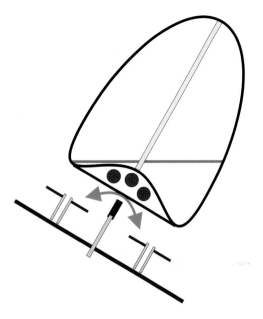

The view from the cockpit during a turn.

Exercise 9b

CLIMBING AND DESCENDING TURNS

The aim of this exercise is to enter and maintain a climb or descent while turning, or to enter and maintain a turn from a straight climb or descent.

You will find during a climbing turn that climb performance (the rate at which the aircraft climbs) is reduced. But during a descending turn the descent rate will increase. Also, in a climbing turn there is an over-bank tendency, meaning that the aircraft will try to tighten and steepen its turn. Conversely, during a descending turn there may be an under-bank tendency with the aircraft trying to roll itself level.

During this exercise you will cover:

Climbing descending turns.

- **A climbing turn**, entered from a straight climb and exiting to a straight climb.

- **A gliding turn**, entered from a straight glide and exiting to a straight glide.

- **A climbing turn**, entered from a level turn and exiting to a level turn.

- **A gliding turn**, entered from a level turn and exiting to a level turn.

During the climbs, monitor the engine temperatures and pressures, and keep a good lookout. During the descents, especially if they are glide descents, keep the engine warm with power bursts every 200–300ft.

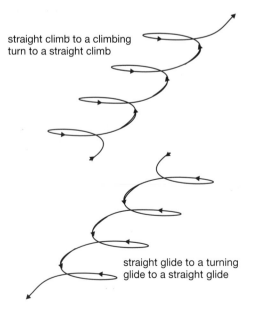

straight climb to a climbing turn to a straight climb

straight glide to a turning glide to a straight glide

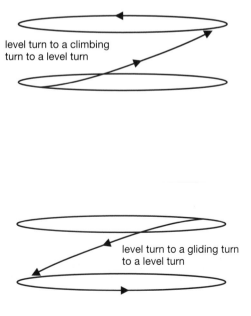

level turn to a climbing turn to a level turn

level turn to a gliding turn to a level turn

Exercise 10a

SLOW FLIGHT

The aims of this exercise are: to become famil-iar with the aircraft in slow flight, just above the stall speed; to recognize the symptoms of the incipient stall; and to restore the aircraft to a safe mode of flight before the stall occurs.

STALL AND STALL SPEED

In steady normal flight, as the airspeed is reduced, the angle of attack must be increased to maintain lift. This will happen whenever airspeed is reduced, regardless of whether the aircraft is climbing or gliding.

If the aircraft is flown too slowly, the angle of attack will exceed the critical angle and the air-flow over the wing will stall. Controlled flight is not possible below this critical speed/angle.

The indications of slow flight are:

- A reduction in airspeed and so of wind pressure on the body (the latter in open-cockpit types, obviously!)

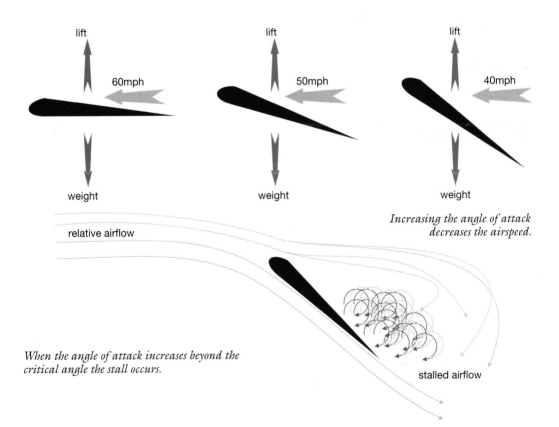

Increasing the angle of attack decreases the airspeed.

When the angle of attack increases beyond the critical angle the stall occurs.

- A reduction in noise due to the reduced airflow
- A possible high-nose attitude – don't confuse the high-nose attitude with a full-power climb
- The control column will be aft of its normal position and the pressure on the control column will be a forwards pressure, i.e. the aircraft is nose heavy and ineffective at pitching up
- The aileron and rudder controls become light and less effective.

Before you try this exercise with your instructor in the air, he should introduce you to a new check: HASELL.

H Height – enough for recovery by now lower than 1,000ft AGL
A Airframe – flaps set as applicable
S Security – seatbelts, helmets, loose articles all secure
E Engine – temperatures and pressures okay
L Location – airspace, wind drift, habitation
L Lookout – clearing turn, looking above and below

The last warning of an approaching stall is the incipient stall, the indications of which are buffeting, severe nose heaviness and lateral instability, i.e. wing drop.

RECOVERY FROM THE INCIPIENT STALL

- Move the control column forward to reduce the angle of attack and simultaneously increase the power to aid acceleration with minimum height loss
- If a wing drops, use opposite rudder to prevent further yaw toward the dropping wing, and then use the above recovery procedure
- Once the speed is safe, return to safe and normal flight, which may mean climbing to a safe height.

Exercise 10b

STALLING

The aim of this exercise is to recognize and enter a fully developed stall in various modes of flight, both straight and turning, and then to recover with minimum height loss to a safe flight mode. Also to recover to a safe flight mode at the incipient stall stage.

The stall occurs whenever the critical angle of attack is exceeded, as shown (*below*). This can happen when:

- Handling mistakes are made
- Flying too slowly
- Pitching up abruptly at speed (high-speed stall)
- With windshear and wind gradient.

A stall results in a decrease in lift and an increase in drag, leading to wing buffet, nose drop and height loss.

THE STALL RECOVERY

Most 3-axis aircraft are naturally stable, and will if left to their own devices recover from a stall by themselves, but this method loses a lot of height. The aircraft will recover from a stall more efficiently if we manage the recovery. There are two types of stall recovery that you will cover with your instructor.

The Pitch-Only Recovery

This type of stall recovery is used when the aircraft is stalled in a full-power climb, or during an engine failure when no power is available. The recovery from a stall using pitch only is to push the control column forward – though not too aggressively – to reduce the angle of attack and un-stall the wing. As soon

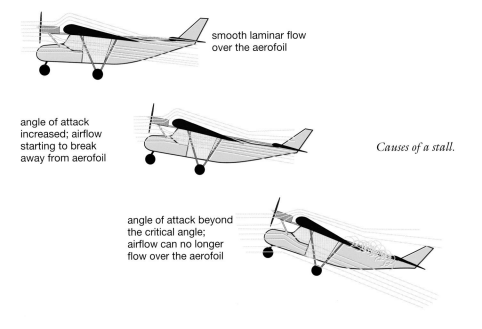

smooth laminar flow over the aerofoil

angle of attack increased; airflow starting to break away from aerofoil

angle of attack beyond the critical angle; airflow can no longer flow over the aerofoil

Causes of a stall.

as a safe airspeed is reached, raise the nose to minimize height loss.

The Standard Stall Recovery

This is used when power is available; the recovery is as follows:

As soon as a safe airspeed is reached, raise the nose to minimize height loss and adopt a shallow climb attitude, and hold to resist a secondary stall. The differences between the two stall recovery methods are better explained by the chart (*bottom*).

You will see from the chart how much height is lost while attempting a pitch-only recovery from a stalled condition, as opposed to a standard stall recovery.

If a wing drops at the stall, un-stall the aircraft in the normal way as described above. During the recovery hold the ailerons in a neutral position and use 'high wing' rudder to prevent further yaw towards the dropping wing. This prevents further yaw developing and stops any chance of the yaw developing into a spin. Take care though, because using excessive rudder before un-stalling the wing may make the other wing drop.

Should the aircraft stall in a turn, use the standard stall recovery, and if the aircraft rolls at the point of the stall use some opposite rudder to resist this.

Don't forget to perform a pre-stall check before attempting any of the stall recoveries. While practising this exercise remember that, as with most flying, this exercise requires co-ordination and understanding. Modern aircraft with their built-in angles of incidence at the tips (washout) are almost self-recovering from a stall: all we pilots are doing is speeding up the recovery process and trying not to lose much height.

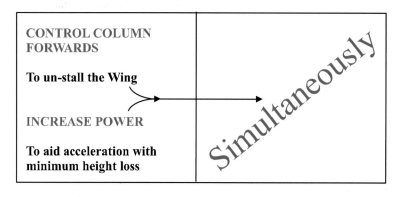

Standard stall recovery.

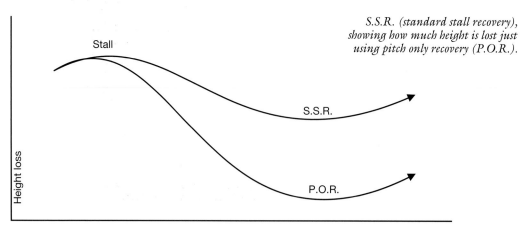

S.S.R. (standard stall recovery), showing how much height is lost just using pitch only recovery (P.O.R.).

Exercise 11

SPIN AWARENESS

The aim of this exercise is to understand and recognize the onset of certain situations that may lead to an inadvertent spin, and to learn how to instinctively take the correct control actions to effect a recovery back to a normal flight condition before a spin occurs; in other words, to recover at the incipient stage.

Since virtually all microlights are not cleared for spinning, this exercise usually takes place in the classroom rather than as a flight exercise, and is thoroughly discussed.

WHAT IS A SPIN?

- A spin is a condition of stalled flight in which the aircraft takes on a spiral descent; if yaw is allowed to occur close to the stall, a spin may develop
- During a spin, the aircraft is stalled, rolling, pitching, sideslipping and very rapidly losing height
- Avoiding the spin means resisting the temptation to pick up a dropping wing with ailerons when close to the stall.

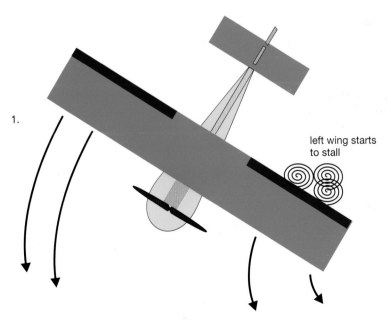

1.

left wing starts to stall

loss of lift and increased drag so wing drops to the left and yaw increases

Spin awareness 1.

Spin awareness 2.

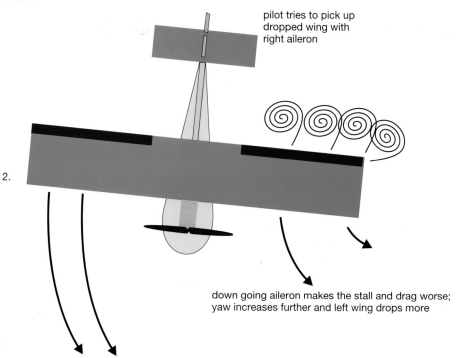

pilot tries to pick up
dropped wing with
right aileron

2.

down going aileron makes the stall and drag worse;
yaw increases further and left wing drops more

Most of the left wing is stalled. The right wing is
still flying. High drag from the left wing causes
the aircraft to rotate to the left. Aircraft is in a
fully developed spin.

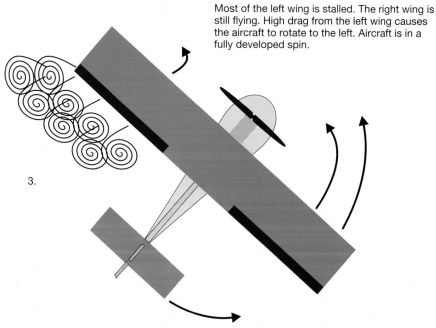

3.

Spin awareness 3.

Exercises 12 and 13

THE TAKE-OFF, CIRCUIT AND LANDING

The aims of this exercise are: to safely take off and climb onto the downwind leg at circuit height; to land the aircraft in the event of an engine failure after take-off or at any other time in the circuit; and to understand when to and be able to abort a take-off should the need arise.

This exercise cannot be fully covered in one flight exercise, and is usually the exercise that students have most of written in their logbooks. It takes a number of briefings and flights: practice makes perfect and plenty of practice will be required to build up your skills to solo standard. So be patient and you will realize that all the previous exercises happen during this 10–15 minute flight: climbing, climbing turns, straight and level, medium-level turns and descending. Along with those exercises you will be taught take-offs and, what is more important, the landing technique.

But first you will have to get used to the circuit. Your first visit to the circuit proper will be over in a flash: everything seems to happen too fast. In fact it doesn't – it is just that there is a lot more pressure than you are used too.

Most circuits are left hand (i.e. always turning to the left), because the pilot in command sits on the left of the aeroplane – this way his/her view of the airfield is unhindered. Some airfields do have right-hand circuits, mainly for noise avoidance and other local bylaws, but for ease I will stick to the left-hand circuit. A typical circuit breaks down as follows:

1. Lined up on the centre line of the runway, all checks complete and ready to roll. Something in the distance to fly towards, and an abort point, chosen, and a rotate speed and a safe climb-out speed in our minds.
2. Once we have applied full power and kept the aircraft in line on the runway, and then

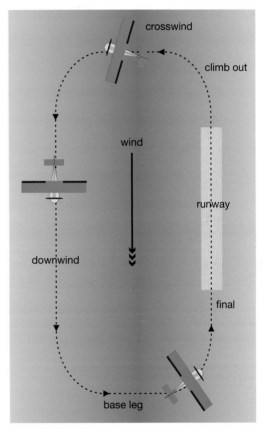

A standard circuit.

rotated (taken off), it is easier to have a relative point to fly towards: pick something static (of course!) in the distance.
3. On climb out we try to keep the airspeed up until we have reached a safe height, typically around 300ft, then we can raise the nose a little more and start a climbing turn onto the crosswind leg.

4. During the crosswind leg you should have reached the circuit height, and should be levelled off at that height. The turn from crosswind to downwind is then a medium-level turn to the left, after you have checked that no-one is joining the downwind leg from your left.

5. Once established on your downwind leg choose another relative point to fly towards: this is the longest leg of the circuit and accurate straight and level flying is a must.

6. About halfway along the downwind leg, we like to do a check (downwind check). I use TWASFUN: T – trim set; W – wind correct for the runway; A – awareness of other traffic in the circuit and on the ground; S – security, i.e. seatbelts, headsets, doors etc; F – fuel enough for a go-round if needed; U – undercarriage, i.e. brakes off; N – needles, i.e. temperatures and pressures okay.

7. We now turn onto the base leg, using a medium-level turn or a descending turn; if it's a descending turn then you have already set up your approach to the runway. The only turn you have left is the turn from base leg to final approach. Your instructor will help you through the latter stages of the approach and landing, but you should follow through to see what inputs are required.

There does seem a lot to take in there, and you will make mistakes: you have to make mistakes to learn, so accept that and accept that these exercises are not an easy two-hour lesson.

THE LANDING

There are three phases to the landing, followed by the ground roll.

The Approach The first phase is the approach. Having achieved a safe approach speed you should be tracking the centreline of the runway, and looking at your chosen touchdown point. Make sure that the nosewheel of the aircraft is straight. If the touchdown point is rising in your line of sight you will land short; if on the other hand it is falling, then you will land long.

The Round-Out At approximately 20ft, ease back on the control column to arrest the descent of the aircraft, and then try to fly the aircraft in a level attitude down the runway with the engine just ticking over. Remember to look all the way to the other end of the runway.

The Hold Off The hold off stage is a combination of reducing the airspeed with pitch input, maintaining the centreline with rudder, until the main undercarriage wheels make contact with the ground.

The Ground Roll

The nosewheel should still be in the air, direction being controlled by rudder. When it wants to, the nosewheel will drop of its own accord. Brake only if necessary.

ENGINE FAILURE

Once you have mastered the circuit and the landing sequence, we pile on the pressure by introducing engine failures during different phases of the of the circuit: EFATO (engine failure after take-off), and engine failure at any point during the circuit.

Landing.

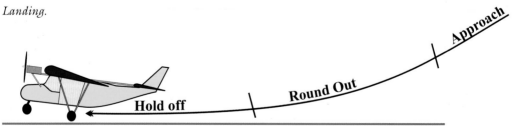

Touchdown

Engine failures during the take-off phase are not common, but because the engine is working at its hardest at that point and the aircraft is close to the ground, and it is travelling only at slow to medium airspeeds, it is imperative that the correct procedure is carried out.

Should an engine failure occur at between 50 and 300ft during take-off, then the only option you have for landing is straight ahead or within 30 degrees of the centreline. A snap decision is required to convert height into airspeed, so that a safe and reasonable landing can be carried out.

Engine failures in the circuit at circuit height are a little less stressful as there is more height available, giving you a little more time to decide where to land. Most airfields are surrounded by flat-ish areas of land, so this should not be a problem. If an engine failure occurs anywhere during the circuit from late downwind, then a landing should be made on the runway in use.

VARIATIONS ON THE CIRCUIT

Your instructor will also demonstrate different take-off and landing techniques, like:

- Crosswind take-offs and landings
- Short-field take-offs and landings
- Soft-field take-offs and landings
- Undulating-field take-offs and landings
- Powered approaches
- Glide to powered approaches.

After you have mastered all the previous phases of this exercise and your instructor is happy, you may be asked if you want to fly your first solo. Technically speaking, 'first solo' is Exercise 17a, so all the previous exercises should have been completed to a satisfactory standard up to and including Exercise 16b, but in some cases it seems the right thing to do at this stage.

JOINING AND LEAVING THE CIRCUIT

Your instructor will also show you how to depart and then re-join the circuit, which should be done as shown in the illustrations (*right and p.96*).

There are certain established etiquettes while flying in the circuit, the most important being **lookout**! Because your workload is so high and because of the possible proximity of other traffic in the circuit, a good lookout is a necessity. Also, microlight aircraft have lower airspeeds than most other aircraft, and flying at different airspeeds in close proximity to one another makes the circuit a prime location for midair collisions.

Make sure on arrival overhead a new airfield that you are fully briefed on the circuit direction, the circuit height (QFE), and any other local rules, and abide by them.

Give way to landing aircraft if you are on the ground, and never assume anything: if you are on final approach and an aircraft starts backtracking down the runway, be prepared to go around, then complain afterwards.

REMEMBER ALL YOUR CHECKS!

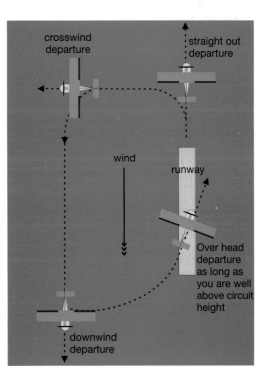

Departing the circuit.

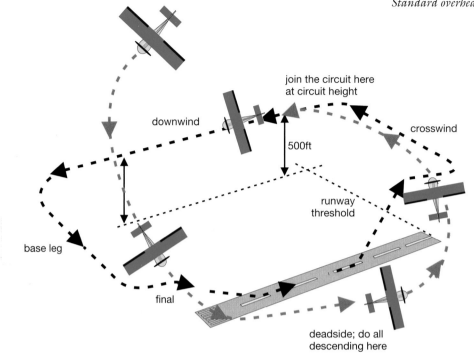

Standard overhead join.

join the circuit here
at circuit height

downwind

crosswind

500ft

runway
threshold

base leg

final

deadside; do all
descending here

Exercise 14

ADVANCED TURNING

The aim of this exercise is to carry out a coordinated level turn at steep angles of bank and to recognize and recover from a spiral dive. It also covers entry and recovery from, and uses of, a side-slipping turn.

During a 60-degree banked level turn, to remain at the same altitude, twice the lift is required compared with that of level flight. To achieve this we must increase the angle of attack (apply back pressure to the control column). This will of course increase drag and in turn reduce airspeed, so we must apply more power.

Also, because the load factor doubles to 2g (twice the force of gravity) at a 60-degree

> During normal flight, power = height and pitch = airspeed.
>
> During a steep turn, power = airspeed and pitch = height.

angle of bank the stall speed increases by 40 per cent. Therefore entry into a steep turn must be made with a good margin of airspeed:

Normal stall speed (Vs) = 34mph
Stall speed at a 60-degree
angle of bank = 47–48mph

Advanced turns.

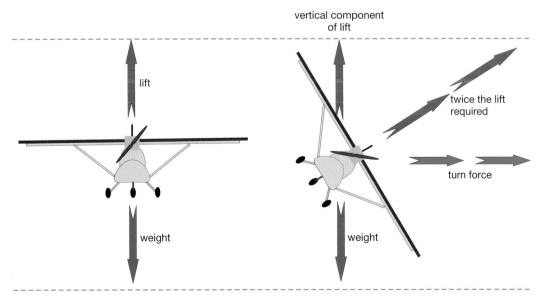

During a steep turn there is a significant wake turbulence produced, so great care must be taken to avoid your own wake turbulence: limit steep turns to 270 degrees.

While climbing steep turns have a big effect on climb rate, so steep turns while climbing are of very little use. On the other hand, steep turns while descending increase the descent rate immensely, so care must be taken while manoeuvring at low level. But it can be used for rapid height loss with dramatic effect. That leads us nicely into spiral dives and the recovery from a spiral dive.

SPIRAL DIVES

Do not confuse a steep descending turn with a spiral dive. A spiral dive is not a controlled descent; it is defined as 'a steep descending turn with the aircraft in an excessively nose-down attitude and with the airspeed increasing rapidly'. Aircraft speed limitations can be rapidly exceeded in a spiral dive.

You must fully understand the associated dangers and how to carry out effective recovery action. You must become familiar with the symptoms of the spiral dive, and its difference from the spin. You can cause a spiral dive by allowing the attitude of the nose to become too low due to excessive bank while in a steep turn. The recovery from a spiral dive is as follows:

1. Close the throttle
2. Level the wings – coordinated control
3. Ease out of the dive
4. Return to a safe mode of flight.

Entry into a steep turn is made as follows:

1. Complete a HASELL check – cockpit checks, minimum altitude, lookout, suitable area.

2. Select a suitable reference point, so you can complete a 270-degree turn.
3. Attain a good entry airspeed; I advocate 5–10mph above Vs + 40 per cent, so if Vs = 34mph then your speed should be 34 + 14mph + 5–10mph = 52–57mph.
4. Have a good lookout before the entry into the turn and roll with coordinated use of aileron and rudder.
5. Centralize roll and yaw inputs when the desired bank angle is achieved; apply back pressure to maintain height or raise the nose attitude slightly.
6. Maintain the bank angle with small roll inputs and balance with the rudder.
7. Maintain height with the elevator; use the horizon or the VSI and the altimeter to gauge height.
8. Maintain airspeed with the use of power and the ASI.

To exit the turn, anticipate the roll-out point and then roll out using coordinated aileron and rudder together. Keep reducing power and relaxing the back pressure on the control column to regain a level flight attitude. Centralize roll inputs when the wings are level with the horizon.

THE SIDESLIP

The sideslip is a useful manoeuvre as it allows us to lose height rapidly without gaining too much airspeed.

The entry is a cross-control of rudder and aileron. Enter a normal gliding turn, then cross the controls by applying out-of-turn rudder while maintaining the bank angle by applying aileron in the direction of turn. This increases drag and so increases descent rate, without a massive increase in airspeed.

Exercise 15

UNUSUAL AND DANGEROUS ATTITUDES/CONDITIONS

The aim of this exercise is to recognize potentially dangerous conditions of flight and recover safely from unusual attitudes. All microlight aircraft have limitations, known as an 'envelope'. Stay within that envelope and mostly the aircraft will behave as it should, but step outside the envelope and bad things will start to happen to the aircraft.

The limitations are:

VNE Velocity never exceed.

VA Manoeuvring speed, the maximum airspeed in turbulent weather.

Maximum bank angle Most microlight aircraft are limited to a 60-degree bank angle.

Maximum pitch angle +/– 30 degrees, some are 45 degrees.

Maximum 'G' loading +4, –2, bits start to fall off beyond these loads.

Manoeuvres at these limits are unusual attitudes, but if left uncorrected may develop into dangerous conditions.

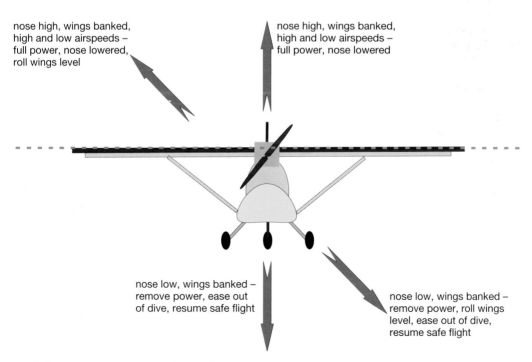

nose high, wings banked, high and low airspeeds – full power, nose lowered, roll wings level

nose high, wings banked, high and low airspeeds – full power, nose lowered

nose low, wings banked – remove power, ease out of dive, resume safe flight

nose low, wings banked – remove power, roll wings level, ease out of dive, resume safe flight

Methods of recovery from unusual attitudes.

Exercise 16a

FORCED LANDINGS WITH AND WITHOUT POWER

The aim of this exercise is to carry out a safe descent, approach and landing in the event of an engine failure during flight, and to carry out a safe unplanned precautionary landing in an unfamiliar field.

Why would an engine fail during flight? Historically, microlights have been prone to engine failures: modern 4-stroke machines are winning the war against engine failures, but even these engines can fail; with that in mind, a pilot has to be able to deal with the scenario. An engine could fail because of:

- Lack of fuel
- Contaminated fuel
- Lack of lubrication
- Mechanical failure
- Pilot shutdown due to mechanical problems.

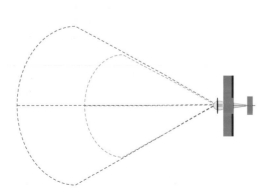

Forced landings.

2,000ft

1,000ft

Be aware at all times during instructional flights that an instructor can spring a simulated engine failure on you at the most inconvenient times. Why? Because engines never fail when we expect them to.

Have a field choice in mind while flying around and be aware of where the wind is from: look for telltale signs such as smoke, high-standing crops, or even lakes. If the lake appears to be calm on one side and rough or rippled on the other, then the wind is coming from the calm side because the bank is sheltering the wind.

You will see from the two illustrations (*left*) that in the event of an engine failure your time in the air and the distance you could possibly travel is dictated by how high you are (based upon still air).

Based upon 500ft per minute minimum sink rate, if you adopted minimum sink from 2,000ft you could have four minutes in the air before you reach the ground, as opposed to two minutes from 1,000ft at the same descent rate.

Once you have adopted this descent rate, your choice of field and where the wind is from dictates where you will attempt to land. A mayday call might be feasible, and you could attempt a restart if time permits. Reassure your passenger if you have one.

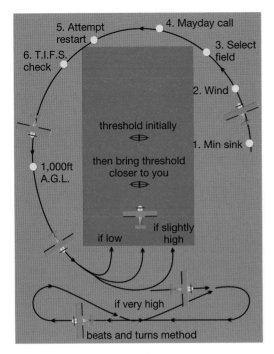

Constant aspect forced landing.

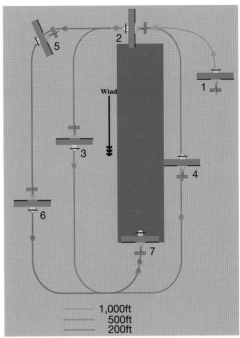

Precautionary landings.

When your engine has failed you also need to complete a series of checks to make sure that you haven't missed anything. I use a TIFS check that covers all you need for an engine failure scenario:

T Throttle off (in case the engine restarts)
I Ignition off
F Fuel tap off
S Seatbelts secure

The illustration below is a typical approach to your chosen field, and when, if time permits, you should attempt the various checks. It also shows what to do if you arrive at the field of your choice too low, too high, very high, or just right. The best way is to give yourself a constant view of your intended landing field. We call this the 'constant aspect method'; this way you can pick a spot in the middle of the field and 'home in' onto it, eventually bringing it nearer to you when on final approach. Never forget that without the engine you can always lose height but you can never get it back – it is always best to be higher rather than lower.

FORCED LANDINGS WITH POWER

The aim of the second part of this exercise is to make an unplanned landing away from an airfield. Why make a precautionary landing?

- Passenger illness
- Deteriorating weather
- You are lost
- Night-time is closing in fast
- Insufficient fuel.

The procedure for this type of forced landing is similar to that of a complete engine failure, except that now we have power. A good check of the field you have in mind is in order, though there is still no time to relax as we have to get the aircraft on the ground quickly.

Having chosen your landing site, make a pass downwind at 1,000ft. If it looks suitable, make another pass using a circuit pattern at 500ft. If it still looks suitable, i.e. if there are no wires, fences, livestock, etc., make another pass at 200ft. This last pass will enable you to see what the surface of the landing site is like – whether it undulates unduly, how long the grass is, and so on. The illustration below will help you to picture the format.

Exercise 16b

OPERATION AT MINIMUM LEVEL

The aim of this exercise is to safely operate the aircraft at heights lower than those normally used. We might need to fly at low level because of lowering cloud perhaps, or to inspect a field in preparation for a precautionary landing. The problems we have in flying low level are the avoidance of military aircraft, Rule 5 of the Air Navigation Order (ANO), and obstacle clearance.

Low flying involving the military takes place between the heights of 250ft and 2,000ft above ground level. During this exercise, if you are flying in an AIAA (Area of Intense Aerial Activity), then a good lookout is a necessity.

Rule 5 of the ANO states that:

• A microlight aircraft shall not fly closer than 500ft to any person, vehicle, vessel or structure, except for the purpose of saving life, taking off or landing in accordance with normal aviation practice

• Also because a microlight operates on a 'Permit to Fly', it must not fly over any congested area of a city, town or settlement.

Things to be aware of while flying low level:

• Obstacles below 300ft are not marked on aeronautical charts
• Always have an active plan for an engine failure: move your track around villages, etc.
• Wind direction
• Low-level turbulence, on the lee side of hills, etc.
• Navigation is more difficult at low level because the reduced height decreases the distance it is possible to see ahead
• Monitor the engine temperatures and pressures, your airspeed and your height.

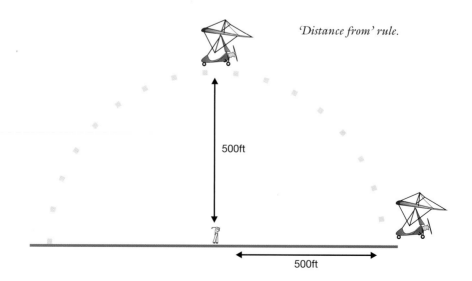

'Distance from' rule.

500ft

500ft

Exercise 17a

FIRST SOLO

The aim of this exercise is to carry out a safe and accurate solo circuit, approach and landing.

As I have said before, the correct time to attempt your first solo is after all the Exercises 1–16b have been satisfactorily completed, but your instructor may have sent you solo after Exercises 12 and 13. Either way, your instructor is looking for good airmanship and the ability to handle situations that could arise with instinct. He is not looking for total perfection, he is looking for safety. With that in mind, the weather will be as near-perfect as it can get, with the wind straight down the runway, and a good, high cloud-base, if any.

Instructors sense and know when a first solo is imminent, but you have to be ready yourself, so don't be afraid to say 'no'.

Before your first solo you must have:

- A medical certificate
- An Airlaw exam pass
- Public liability insurance (check with your instructor).

Most of all, enjoy: after your first solo, the feeling of what you have accomplished never leaves you, but the moment does. Pat yourself on the back after everyone has shaken your hand, because technically you are now a pilot.

All my students do three circuits on their first solo: one at normal circuit height, without an attempt to land, to get used to the aircraft without an instructor in it; one with an approach down to 200ft followed by a go-around; then a normal circuit with, hopefully, a landing at the end of it.

Exercise 17b

SOLO CIRCUIT, GENERAL FLYING

The aim of this exercise is to practise and polish the skills learned during the dual training, and to prepare for the General Flying Test.

Usually your instructor will get in the aircraft with you to check you are still operating the aircraft and yourself in a competent manner – we call these 'check flights'. Don't be upset or surprised if permission to fly solo is refused: the weather needs to be near-perfect for your early solo work. As you gain more and more experience the weather window will expand.

You will be asked to practise differing take-off and landing techniques. You will also be asked to practise, when the circuit traffic permits, PFLs (practice forced landings) from 1,000ft overhead the airfield.

As time advances you will eventually 'break circuit' and do some local flying away from the airfield, practising the departure and rejoining methods. During these trips you may fly a triangular route that your instructor has prepared for you. Map reading, identification of local features and maintaining a compass heading are all the more important now.

You will also review the basics on your own general handling skills. I provide my students with a 'solo consolidation card' that lists various tasks to do while flying.

Exercise 17c

DUAL REVISION FOR GFT

The aim of this exercise is to correct any bad habits that may have formed during your solo work, and to check that no aspect of your training has been overlooked.

This will usually take more than one session, and I like to do a 'mock' GFT to see how a student copes. There is also a ground oral aircraft technical exam, which covers rigging, de-rigging, preparation for flight, fuel and maintenance requirements, and full knowledge of the aircraft's systems and their operation.

NB: Exercise 18 (Navigation), which is identical for both 3-axis and weight-shift aircraft, is to be found at the end of the weight-shift section, on page 136.

The Weight-Shift Microlight Syllabus

Exercise 1. Aircraft Familiarization

Exercise 2. Preparation for Flight and Action After

Exercise 3. Air Experience

Exercise 4. Effects of Controls

Exercise 5. Taxying

Exercise 6. Straight and Level

Exercise 7. Climbing

Exercise 8. Descending

Exercise 9a. Medium-Level Turns (up to 30 Degrees of Bank)

Exercise 9b. Climbing and Descending Turns

Exercise 10a. Slow Flight

Exercise 10b. Stalling

Exercise 11.
(Not applicable to weight-shift aircraft)

Exercise 12. Take-Off and Climb to Downwind

Exercise 13. The Circuit, Approach and Landing/Overshoot

Exercise 14. Advanced Turns (up to and including 60 Degrees of Bank)

Exercise 15. Unusual Attitudes

Exercise 16a. Forced Landings, with/without Power

Exercise 16b. Operation at Minimum Level

Exercise 17a. First Solo

Exercise 17b. Solo Circuit, General Flying

Exercise 17c. Dual Revision for GFT

Exercise 18. Navigation

Weight-shift aircraft differ from other aircraft types in the way that they are controlled. Being derived from hang-glider technology, they use the combined weight of the trike (the place where the pilot sits) and the occupants to manoeuvre the aircraft around in the air. The controls are very basic: a control bar and a throttle.

The control bar is attached to the wing rigidly with nuts, bolts and wires: move the bar, and you move the wing. Push the bar away from you and the nose of the wing will point upwards (angle of attack increases), pull the bar towards you and the nose of the wing will point downwards (angle of attack decreases). Move the bar to the left and the right wingtip will move downward and the left wingtip will move upward; move the bar to the right and the left wingtip will move downward and the right wingtip will go upward … simple!

Depress the throttle with your right foot and the engine will run faster, release your right foot from the throttle and the engine will run slower … simple!

Using a combination of these controls we can make the aircraft do almost anything in the air, within its limitations. We can make the aircraft climb, descend, turn and, of course, combine some of those together in manoeuvres such as climbing and descending turns.

The syllabus for a full NPPL(M) licence requires a minimum instructional period of twenty-five hours. Ten of these hours must be solo and must include five hours' navigation training, where two solo cross-country flights are completed. A restricted licence requires a minimum instructional period of fifteen hours, of which seven must be solo.

Exercises 1, 2 and 3

These first exercises are usually taken as an air-experience flight, and consist of you – the student – taking to the air with an instructor at the school of your choice.

Exercise 1 is aircraft familiarization, finding out the different parts that make up the aircraft and where you will sit while flying, and being given a general brief on safety aspects.

Exercise 2 is preparing the aircraft for flight, refuelling if necessary, pre-flight checks, and learning where you will be flying and at what heights.

Exercise 3 is the actual air-experience flight, your chance to fly the aircraft and experience the feeling of flying. Generally these flights are of twenty to sixty minutes' duration.

Many flying clubs arrange air-experience flights, so you can have a go before committing yourself to a course of flying lessons.

Exercise 4

EFFECTS OF CONTROLS

The aim of this exercise is to understand how each control affects the aircraft during flight. Exercise 4 is the basis of all your flying training: learning anything new starts with the foundation, so get to grips with this exercise and the rest of your training will follow easily.

Your instructor should at this point have told you how each flight during your training will be handled and, what is more important, how control is handed over between you and him. Generally the conversation goes like this: (instructor) 'You have control'; (student) 'I have control', and vice versa.

During this lesson you will learn how to assess the aircraft's attitude from outside references such as the horizon and the feel of the wind pressure on your body. You will be shown that the aircraft will virtually fly itself: all aircraft 'know' how to fly, the main problem with weight-shift aircraft being that they don't know where to go. While they are

inherently stable in pitch and roll, their directional stability leaves a lot to be desired.

To assess the aircraft's attitude with the horizon, try to align the base bar with the horizon and try to keep the front strut at 90 degrees to the horizon, as in the illustration below.

Another method is to keep each wingtip equidistant from the horizon. From where you sit, it looks like approximately 2–3ft (60–100cm) above the horizon. We need a datum to work from for all the exercises. All these tips will help you keep the aircraft the right way up and fairly straight.

During Exercise 4 you will also look at each control in turn, find out what it does and what happens if you keep applying that input; these are called primary effects and secondary effects. You will also learn the effect airspeed has on the controls: the faster we travel through the air the more responsive the controls are, while when we are flying slower the

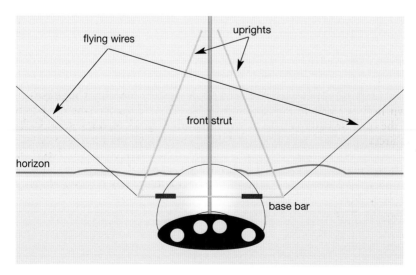

The view from a trike seat during flight.

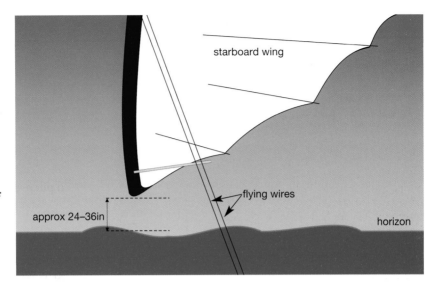

RIGHT: During normal flight each wing should be equidistant from the horizon!

BELOW: Weight-shift aircraft have two axes of movement, lateral and longitudinal.

BELOW RIGHT: The controls on a weight-shift aircraft.

starboard wing

flying wires

horizon

approx 24–36in

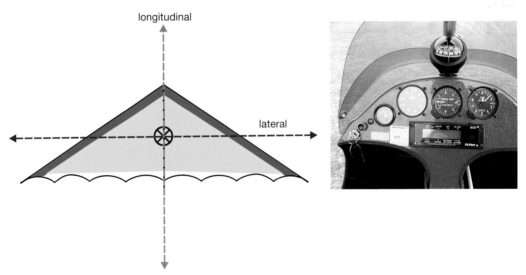

longitudinal

lateral

controls become sloppy and unresponsive. You will also be shown how slipstream and engine torque affects the aircraft. The controls on a weight-shift aircraft are:

- Pitch, which controls airspeed
- Roll, which controls turns
- Power, which controls height
- Trim, which is ancillary to these.

Airmanship should always play a large part of flying and this will be drummed into you even at this very early stage. Keeping a good look-out and demonstrating good engine management have to be instinctive so don't be surprised if you are told many times to look out before you attempt any manoeuvre.

Exercise 5

TAXYING

This exercise, although important, doesn't warrant a whole lesson on its own. Therefore every lesson you do will incorporate taxying in it somewhere – that is, unless you are going to push the aircraft to the runway!

The weight-shift aircraft is very susceptible to wind on the ground: because of its large sail area, winds can quite easily get underneath the wing, rip the bar out of your hands and flip the whole aircraft onto its side. To avoid this you will be shown how to taxi in a crosswind, headwind and tailwind. You will be shown the correct taxying speed, which is usually a fast walking pace, unless you have to vacate the runway urgently.

If the wind is from your left as you are taxying, then move the bar to the right, drop the left wingtip down and hold it there.

If the wind is from the right then drop the right wing down. (You only need to be slightly down with each wingtip, or else you will be dragging the tips on the ground. Dropping each tip into the wind has the effect of making the wind travel up the sail rather than under it.)

If the wind is from behind then the bar needs to be pushed toward the front strut, which again helps the wind travel over the top of the sail.

If the wind is from the front then bias the wing slightly nose down, unless you are about to take off.

If the wind is any combination of the above then adjust the wing accordingly. For example, if the wind is from behind and from the left you should keep the left wingtip down and the bar pushed towards the front strut.

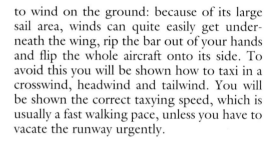

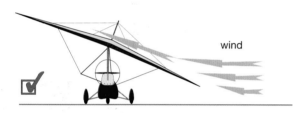

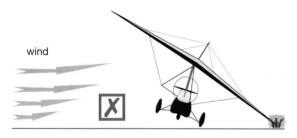

Exercise 6

STRAIGHT AND LEVEL

This exercise, one of my favourite, aims to teach you how to maintain straight-line flight at a constant altitude, and also how to maintain straight-line flight at a constant altitude at differing airspeeds. During this exercise you will learn than you need to be coordinated, by use of the power and the pitch control.

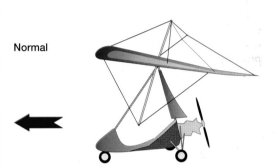

Normal

LOOKOUT is of paramount importance during this exercise, because you will tend to be concentrating on the instruments.

Your instructor will give you a visual bearing to fly toward, and if you aren't knocked off track by the weather then the instructor will knock the aircraft off track for you.

The use of hands-off trim (letting go of the control bar) will be shown to demonstrate the aircraft's inherent stability in roll and pitch, using the altimeter and the VSI (if fitted) to check any fluctuations in height.

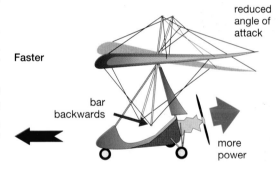

Faster

reduced angle of attack

bar backwards

more power

REMEMBER :

Power = Height, and Pitch = Airspeed.

When you have competently flown the aircraft in a straight line at a constant altitude, your instructor will introduce you to doing the same at differing airspeeds. This is where coordination is necessary.

To fly faster than hands-off trim we need to increase power slightly, then stop the aircraft from climbing by changing the angle of attack

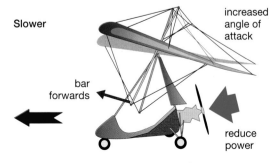

Slower

increased angle of attack

bar forwards

reduce power

of the wing. Pulling the bar towards you will stop the aircraft climbing and will increase your airspeed, then all you have to do is keep on a constant heading using roll control and maintain a constant height with subtle use of the power – the pitch control is used to control the airspeed.

To return to normal flight (hands-off trim), first you reduce the power back to the normal power setting, then slowly relax the forward pressure on the bar (bar back), still maintaining your heading.

To fly slower than 'hands off trim' you need to reduce the power slightly, then stop the aircraft descending by increasing the angle of attack. Pushing the bar away from you increases the angle of attack, and stops the plane descending as you reduce the airspeed.

There is backwards pressure on the bar now and the controls may feel sloppy due to the reduced airspeed. Maintain your height with power and your airspeed with the pitch control and maintain your heading with the roll control.

To return to normal flight from slower flight, increase the power to just beyond normal cruise power, then slowly let the pressure relax on the bar until all the pressure is gone (bar forward). Return the power back to normal and maintain your heading using roll control.

Exercise 7

CLIMBING

The aim of this exercise is to enter and maintain a steady full-power climb, in a straight line, and then to return to level flight at a predetermined altitude. This is the basis for all climbs, be they full-power, cruise or best rate climbs. Full-power climbs, obviously, are climbs using full engine power, and are usually used for take-off and other circumstances where maximum rate of climb for a given flight attitude is needed. Cruise climbs are climbs with no loss in airspeed but a slight decrease in engine power, usually used to keep the engine from over-heating. Best rate climbs are climbs that use the full power of the aircraft and as much pitch input as is possible.

The four forces during normal flight are as shown in the picture below. When thrust equals drag and lift equals weight there will be no speed increase and no climb or descent. We have already ascertained that power equals height, so surely to climb all we need to do is increase the power? In theory that's fine for today's high-powered machines, but we still like to make the aircraft climb by converting speed into height. We use a mnemonic for climbing, PAHT:

P Power
A Attitude
H Hold
T Trim

So we apply power, a surge of airspeed, then we change the attitude and hold that attitude,

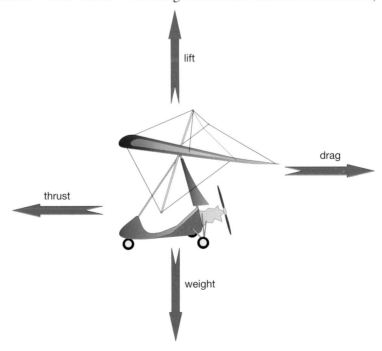

The forces.

then we trim for the airspeed we want to climb at. This will show you that by combining power and attitude you can maintain a set performance in climb rate and airspeed.

To enable the aircraft and its occupants to climb, more power is needed to balance the increase in drag from the weight. Drag also varies with airspeed, so climbing performance will also vary with different airspeeds.

This is the basis for all climbs, be they full-power climbs, cruise climbs, or best rate climbs. The item that alters is the trim: you can decide

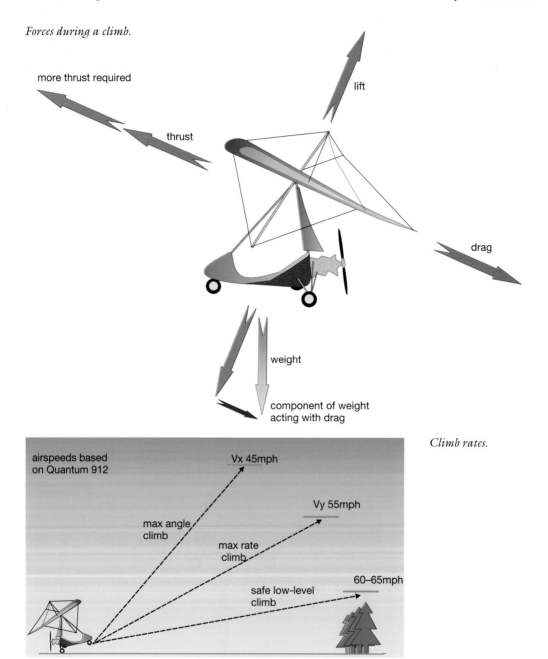

Forces during a climb.

more thrust required

thrust

lift

drag

weight

component of weight acting with drag

Climb rates.

airspeeds based on Quantum 912

Vx 45mph

max angle climb

Vy 55mph

max rate climb

safe low-level climb

60–65mph

the climb rate you want by selecting differing airspeeds, but remember that it is always power first, then an attitude change, then decide what climb rate you want.

When you have reached the top of your climb you will need to level off. To do this we change the attitude first (which increases the airspeed), then we reduce the power; removing the power first would seriously reduce the airspeed because the wing is already at a higher angle of attack than normal. Therefore:

A Attitude change first
H Hold the attitude, to increase airspeed
P Power – reduce back to normal cruise power
T Trim – revert to hands-off trim

Your instructor will show you differing climb rates; these are achieved by altering the airspeed during the climb.

Airmanship plays a big part in this exercise as weight-shift aircraft have a massive blind spot: the wing is in the way of seeing if any other traffic is above you, so a good lookout is imperative before you attempt any climb.

Always pick a bearing to fly towards, so that you keep in a straight line while climbing. During a climb constantly check the engine temperatures and pressures: the engine is working hard and needs to be monitored.

Exercise 8

DESCENDING

What goes up must come down, so you must be able to descend the aircraft with control and safety, and of course to stop the descent and level off when needed. The aim of this exercise is to enter and maintain a steady glide descent, in a straight line, and then at a pre-determined altitude return to level flight or enter a climb; also to enter and maintain a steady cruise descent, in a straight line.

The forces in normal flight are as below: lift equals weight, thrust equals drag. When we need to descend the aircraft, we know that power controls height, so simply removing the power will make the aircraft descend.

However, the secondary effect of removing power is a reduction in airspeed, so we need to increase the airspeed before we start a descent. We use the mnemonic AHPT.

A   Attitude first
H   Hold to increase airspeed
P   Reduce the power
T   Trim for desired airspeed

During a glide descent, a component of weight adds to the thrust or takes its place. Your instructor will demonstrate that differing airspeeds will give you differing descent rates.

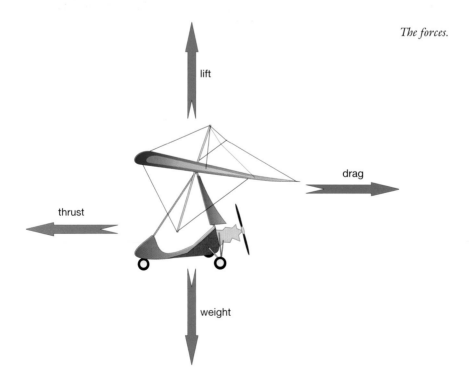

The forces.

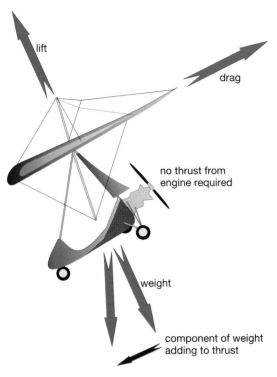

lift

drag

no thrust from
engine required

weight

component of weight
adding to thrust

Forces during descent.

Once you have reached your desired altitude or height you will need to level off to continue at that height/altitude. We use the same mnemonic, but rearrange the order: (P&A) HT.

(P&A) Power and attitude together arrests the descent decisively and abruptly, but be aware that if you are close to the ground the attitude change must precede the power increase by a small margin

H Hold the attitude to increase the airspeed

T Trim to your desired airspeed, usually hands-off trim

Your instructor will demonstrate cruise descents and glide descents. Cruise descents are made with a small amount of power kept on, and are good for keeping the engine warm. Glide descents are made with the engine throttled right back to idling power, and you must remember that during a glide descent the engine can cool down very quickly, so keep increasing the rpm periodically – say every 200–300ft – to maintain engine warmth.

Exercise 9a

MEDIUM-LEVEL TURNS

The aim of this exercise is to enter and maintain a medium-level turn (up to 30 degrees of bank) while maintaining level flight, then to return to straight and level flight on a new heading.

During a 30-degree bank turn more lift is required to maintain level flight: due to the bank, some of the lift is no longer counter-acting weight, so without an increase in lift the aircraft will slip into the turn and descend. More lift can be produced by increasing the angle of attack, though this will reduce the airspeed, by approximately 5mph. Power can be used if necessary to maintain airspeed.

Maintaining the turn is a simple matter of using the aircraft's inbuilt structures in rela-tion to the horizon. With practice, you will be able to gauge when the front strut is at 30 degrees to the horizon. The other method is to use the lower wing in relation to the hori-zon: keep the wing wires on or near the hori-zon, the perfect way to judge a 30-degree bank turn.

Monitor the height with the VSI and the altimeter, and also monitor the airspeed – if the airspeed drops too much, increase the rpm and relax a little on the bar.

Remember that all-important airmanship. Endlessly going round and round in circles is disorienting; before starting any turn have a good lookout in the direction of turn, and

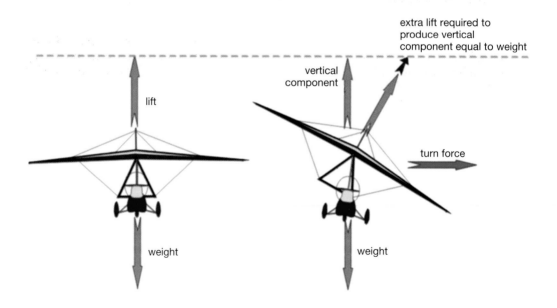

lift

weight

extra lift required to produce vertical component equal to weight

vertical component

turn force

weight

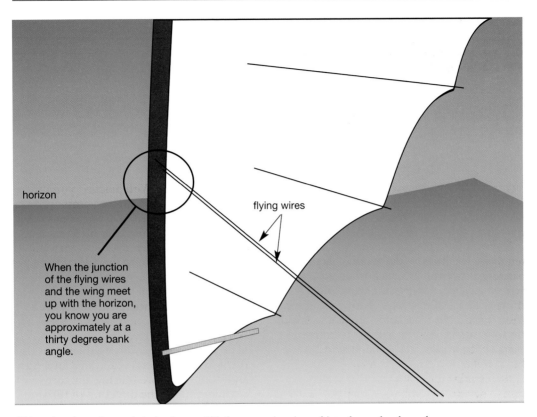

horizon

flying wires

When the junction of the flying wires and the wing meet up with the horizon, you know you are approximately at a thirty degree bank angle.

Using the wing wire and the horizon will help you maintain a thirty degree bank angle.

all around, and while turning look into the turn to make sure that the way is clear.

It is much easier to roll out of the turn on a feature on the ground than by using the compass. If your instructor says '360 degrees all the way round', take a mental note of what is in front of you and look for it on the way round. Anticipate the roll-out and you will hit the heading every time.

Exercise 9b

CLIMBING AND DESCENDING TURNS

The aim of this exercise is to enter and maintain a climb or descent while turning, or to enter and maintain a turn from a straight climb or descent.

You will find that if you start to turn while climbing, the bank angle has to be kept quite shallow otherwise your climb performance will be affected. Usually the bank angle is no more than 15–20 degrees. During a climbing turn there is an over-bank tendency, which means that the aircraft will try to tighten its turn, so bank angle has to be 'held off'.

On the other hand, if you start to turn while descending, then the steeper you turn the more the descent rate increases. During a descending turn there may be an under-bank tendency, which means that the aircraft will try to roll itself level: bank angle has to be 'held on'.

During this exercise you will cover:

- A climbing turn, entered from a straight climb and exiting to a straight climb
- A gliding turn, entered from a straight glide and exiting to a straight glide
- A climbing turn, entered from a level turn and exiting to a level turn
- A gliding turn, entered from a level turn and exiting to a level turn.

Entry into a climbing turn is a fairly simple matter. After the necessary lookout, enter a normal full-power climb and then initiate a right or left turn; use no more than 15–20 degrees angle of bank, making sure your airspeed is within safe margins.

To level off at a predetermined altitude still in a turn is exactly the same as levelling off normally, the only difference being that the turn stays in. Remember, though, that as you level off during a turn the bank angle may want to increase, so be ready to check the bank angle.

Entry into a descending turn is also fairly routine. First enter a descent, then add bank angle in the direction you wish to turn. Your VSI (if fitted) will show that your descent rate is more than during a normal descent. The steeper the bank angle during a descending turn, the better the descent rate. Most of our descending turns and climbing turns are made during the take-off and landing phases of flight, so good coordination and awareness of airspeed is required by the end of this exercise.

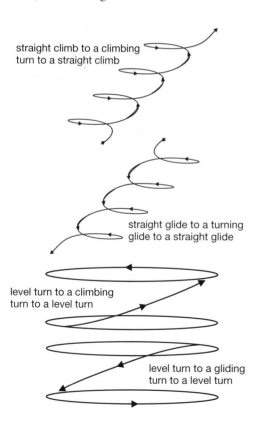

straight climb to a climbing turn to a straight climb

straight glide to a turning glide to a straight glide

level turn to a climbing turn to a level turn

level turn to a gliding turn to a level turn

Exercise 10a

SLOW FLIGHT

The aims of this exercise are: to become familiar with the aircraft in slow flight, just above the stall speed; to recognize the symptoms of the incipient stall; and to restore the aircraft to a safe mode of flight before the stall occurs.

STALL AND STALL SPEED

In steady normal flight, as the airspeed is reduced, the angle of attack must be increased to maintain lift. This will happen whenever airspeed is reduced, regardless of whether the aircraft is climbing or gliding.

If the aircraft is flown too slowly, the angle of attack will exceed the critical angle and the airflow over the wing will stall. Controlled flight is not possible below this critical speed/angle.

The indications of slow flight are:

- A reduction in airspeed and so of wind pressure on the body

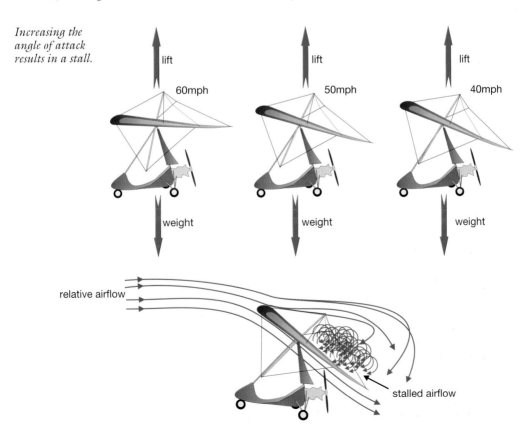

Increasing the angle of attack results in a stall.

lift   60mph   weight

lift   50mph   weight

lift   40mph   weight

relative airflow

stalled airflow

- A reduction in noise due to the reduced airflow
- A possible high-nose attitude – don't confuse the high-nose attitude with a full-power climb.
- The bar will have a tremendous amount of rearwards pressure (trying to force the bar back to the pilot)
- The roll and pitch controls become sloppy and unresponsive.

Before you attempt the slow-flight exercise you must complete a HASELL check because you will be flying the aircraft at or near the incipient stall, which is the last warning of an approaching stall.

The incipient stall means that the aircraft is still flying, just. There could be buffeting of the wing, severe nose-heaviness and wing drop: the aircraft just wants to fall out of the sky. The recovery from the incipient stall is as follows:

- Bar back to reduce the angle of attack
- Increase power simultaneously to aid acceleration with minimum height loss.

Exercise 10b

STALLING

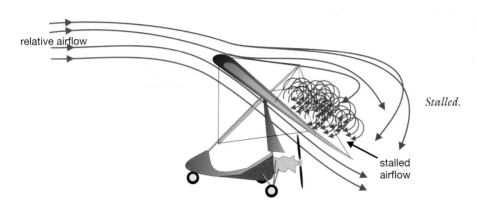

relative airflow

Stalled.

stalled
airflow

The aim of this exercise is to recognize and enter a fully developed stall in various modes of flight, both straight and turning, and then to recover with minimum height loss to a safe flight mode. Also to recover to a safe flight mode at the incipient stall stage.

The stall occurs whenever the critical angle of attack is exceeded, as shown above. This can happen when:

- Handling mistakes are made
- Flying too slowly
- Pitching up abruptly at speed (high-speed stall)
- With windshear and wind gradient.

A stall results in a decrease in lift and an increase in drag, leading to wing buffet, nose drop and height loss.

STALL RECOVERY

As discussed before, weight-shift aircraft are inherently stable in both roll and pitch. They have an inbuilt washout that helps the aircraft to self-recover even if you do nothing at all to the controls. Self-recovery (leaving the aircraft to its own devices) does have a serious disadvantage: drastic height loss. The aircraft will recover more effectively if we manage the recovery, and to this end you will be shown the 'pitch-only recovery' and the 'standard stall recovery'.

The pitch-only recovery is used when the aircraft is stalled in a full-power climb, or when there is no power available. The recovery is as follows: bar back, to reduce the angle of attack, but not too aggressively; when a safe airspeed is reached, raise the nose to try to minimize height loss.

The height loss is minimized if we manage the recovery using power, with the standard stall recovery (*see* diagram p.124, *top*).

When a safe airspeed is reached, raise the nose to minimize height loss and adopt a shallow climb attitude and hold to resist a secondary stall.

WHAT IS A SECONDARY STALL?

This stall is called a secondary stall since it may occur after a recovery from a preceding 'primary' stall. It is caused by attempting to hasten the completion of a stall recovery before the aircraft has regained sufficient flying speed

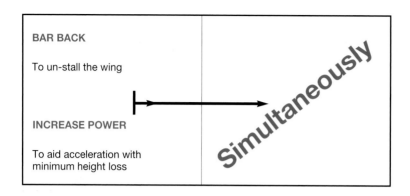

BAR BACK

To un-stall the wing

INCREASE POWER

To aid acceleration with
minimum height loss

Simultaneously

This stall usually occurs when the pilot becomes too anxious in returning to straight and level flight after a stall.

THE STALL

By the end of this exercise you should have a reasonable level of competence in all general flying skills. You should be able to control the aircraft safely in slow flight, and be able to recover the aircraft at the incipient stall stage. You will probably recap on many of the previous exercises at this stage; this is normal practice, to consolidate your training and make sure you haven't forgotten the all-important basics.

Always remember that microlight flying is weather-dependent and that a good continuity of training is paramount. Leaving three or four weeks between lessons doesn't do you or your bank balance any favours, since you might have to recap the previous lesson before you can move on to the next.

It is time now to move on to the next stage of your training, when all the previous exercises happen in one flight: the circuit.

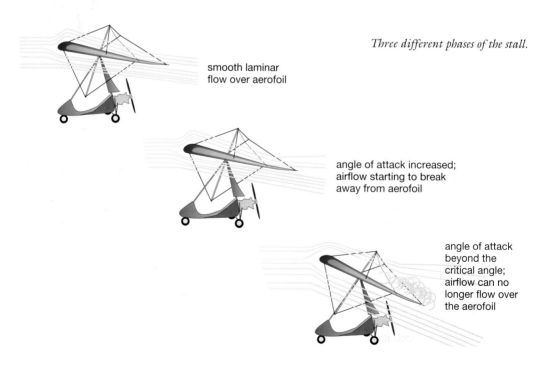

Three different phases of the stall.

smooth laminar
flow over aerofoil

angle of attack increased;
airflow starting to break
away from aerofoil

angle of attack
beyond the
critical angle;
airflow can no
longer flow over
the aerofoil

Exercises 12 and 13

THE TAKE-OFF, CIRCUIT AND LANDING

The aims of the first part of this exercise, Exercise 12, are: to safely take off and climb onto the downwind leg at circuit height; to land the aircraft in the event of an engine failure after take-off or at any other time in the circuit; and to understand when to and be able to abort a take-off should the need arise. The second part of the exercise, Exercise 13, is to fly an accurate circuit and carry out a safe approach and landing.

This exercise cannot be fully covered in one flight exercise, and is usually the exercise that students have most of written in their logbooks. It takes a number of briefings and flights: practice makes perfect and plenty of practice will be required to build up your skills to solo standard.

Most circuits are left hand (i.e. always turning to the left), because the pilot in command sits on the left of the aeroplane – this way his/her view of the airfield is unhindered. Some airfields do have right-hand circuits, mainly for noise avoidance and other local bylaws, but for ease I will stick to the left-hand circuit. The standard circuit has five sections:

- Climb out
- Crosswind leg
- Downwind leg
- Base leg
- Final.

The circuit is flown in a rectangular shape with the downwind leg parallel to the runway, as shown in the diagram (*right*).

A typical circuit breaks down as follows:

1. Lined up on the centreline of the runway, all checks complete and ready to roll. Something in the distance to fly towards, and an abort point, chosen, and a rotate speed and a safe climb-out speed in our minds.

2. Once we have applied full power and kept the aircraft in line on the runway, and then rotated (taken off), it is easier to have a relative point to fly towards: pick something static (of course!) in the distance.

3. On climb out we try to keep the airspeed up until we have reached a safe height, typi-

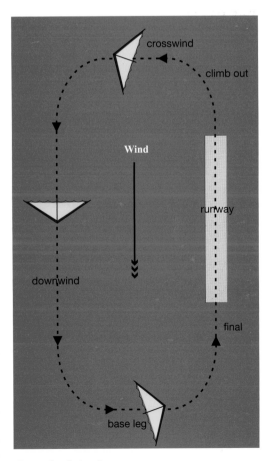

A standard circuit.

cally around 300ft, then we can raise the nose a little more and start a climbing turn onto the crosswind leg.

4. During the crosswind leg you should have reached the circuit height, and should be levelled off at that height. The turn from crosswind to downwind is then a medium-level turn to the left, after you have checked that no-one is joining the downwind leg from your left.

5. When you are established on your downwind leg choose another relative point to fly towards: this is the longest leg of the circuit and accurate straight and level flying is a must.

6. About halfway along the downwind leg, we like to do a 'downwind check'; I use FAWNTS: F – fuel enough for a go-round if needed; A – awareness of other traffic in the circuit and on the ground; W – wind correct for runway; N – needles (temperatures and pressures) okay, nosewheel straight; T – hand throttle is off; S – security, i.e. seatbelts.

7. We now turn onto the base leg, using a medium-level turn or a descending turn; if it's a descending turn then you have already set up your approach to the runway. The only turn you have left is the turn from base leg to final approach. Your instructor will help you through the latter stages of the approach and landing, but you should follow through to see what inputs are required.

There does seem a lot to take in there, and you will make mistakes: you have to make mistakes to learn, so accept that and accept that these exercises are not an easy two-hour lesson.

THE LANDING

There are three phases to the landing:

The Approach The first phase is the approach. Having achieved a safe approach speed you should be tracking the centreline of the runway, and looking at your chosen touchdown point. Make sure that the nosewheel of the aircraft is straight. If the touchdown point is rising in your line of sight you will land short; if on the other hand it is falling, then you will land long.

The Round-Out At approximately 20ft we have to arrest our descent, or else we will hit the runway. If you are holding back pressure on the base bar, relax that pressure, or gently push the base bar away from you. A small amount will be sufficient: too much, and you will be heading skyward again. You need to end up in a level attitude approximately 2–3ft (60–90cm) above the ground.

The Hold Off The hold off is a combination of reducing the airspeed with pitch input and maintaining the centreline with roll input until the main wheels make contact with the ground. The ground roll is a simple matter of keeping the aircraft straight and using brake if necessary.

Once you have mastered the circuit and handled some emergencies like EFATO (engine failure after take-off), aborted take-offs and engine failures in the circuit, your instructor will move on to differing take-offs and landings. These involve dealing with crosswinds and short fields. There are many techniques you will need such as:

Landing.

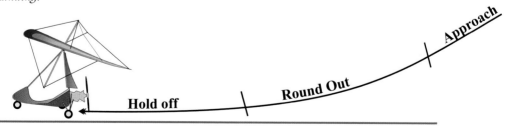

- Crosswind take-off and landings
- Short-field take-off and landings
- Soft-field take-off and landings
- Undulating field take-off and landings
- Powered approaches
- Glide to powered approaches.

Your instructor will also demonstrate how to depart the circuit and then rejoin the circuit, using your local airfield rules.

It is very important that you maintain a good lookout while in the circuit. The workload may be high, but so is the number of other aircraft in very close proximity to each other, and you should never assume that another aircraft has seen you.

Many of you might wonder: 'If I can land the aircraft can I do my first solo?' The short answer is technically 'no', you should have completed to a satisfactory standard all the exercises up to and including Exercise 16b.

There would be times during most student's training that the circuit wasn't suitable for training on that day, and the other remaining exercises are completed then. My personal view is that all the Exercises 1 through to 16b should be completed before any attempt is made to go solo.

Exercise 14

ADVANCED TURNS

The aim of this exercise is to carry out a coordinated level turn at steep angles of bank and to recognize and recover from a spiral dive. It also covers entry and recovery from, and uses of, a side-slipping turn.

During a 60-degree banked level turn, twice the lift is required compared with that of level flight. To achieve this we must increase the angle of attack (move the bar forwards). This will of course increase drag and in turn reduce airspeed, so we must apply more power.

> During normal flight, power = height and pitch = airspeed.
>
> During a steep turn, power = airspeed and pitch = height.

Also, because the load factor doubles to 2g (twice the force of gravity) at a 60-degree angle of bank, the stall speed increases by 40 per cent. Therefore entry into a steep turn must be made with a good margin of airspeed:

Normal stall speed (Vs) = 34mph
Stall speed at a 60-degree angle of bank = 47mph

During a steep turn there is a significant wake turbulence produced, so great care must be taken to avoid your own wake turbulence: limit steep turns to 270 degrees.

You will find out that if you introduce a climb during a steep turn the climb rate will be virtually non-existent, while on the other hand steep turns while descending increase descent rate immensely, so therefore care

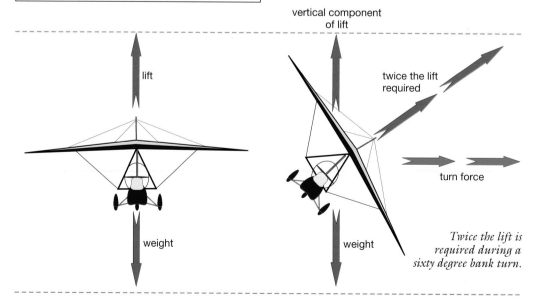

vertical component of lift

lift

weight

twice the lift required

turn force

weight

Twice the lift is required during a sixty degree bank turn.

270 degrees only during steep turns.

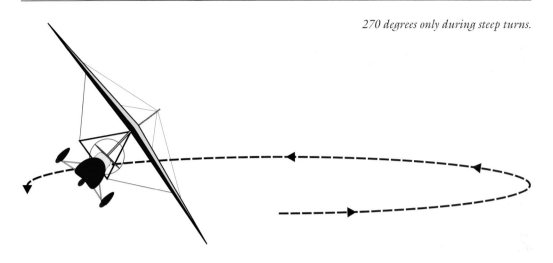

must be taken at low levels. This leads us nice-ly into spiral dives.

SPIRAL DIVES

Do not confuse a steep descending turn with a spiral dive. A spiral dive is not a controlled descent; it is defined as 'a steep descending turn with the aircraft in an excessively nose-down attitude and with the airspeed increasing rapidly'. Aircraft speed limitations can be rapidly exceeded in a spiral dive.

You must fully understand the associated dangers and how to carry out effective recovery action. You can cause a spiral dive by allowing the attitude of the nose to become too low due to excessive bank while in a steep turn. The recovery from a spiral dive is as follows:

1. Close the throttle.
2. Level the wings – coordinated control.
3. Ease out of the dive.
4. Return to a safe mode of flight.

Entry into a steep turn is made as follows:

1. Complete a HASELL check – cockpit checks, minimum altitude, lookout, suit-able area.
2. Select a suitable reference point, so you can complete a 270-degree turn.
3. Attain a good entry airspeed; I advocate

5–10mph above Vs + 40 per cent, so if Vs = 34mph then your speed should be 34 + 14mph + 5–10mph = 52–57mph.
4. Have a good lookout before the entry into the turn, roll into the turn applying pitch input to maintain height and maintaining the bank angle with small roll inputs.
5. As the drag increases due to large pitch inputs, apply power to maintain airspeed.
6. Maintain height with pitch input, using the horizon or the VSI and the altimeter.
7. Maintain airspeed with the use of power and the ASI.

To exit the turn, anticipate the roll-out point and start to roll out of the turn. Keep reducing power and relaxing the pressure on the base bar to regain a level flight attitude. Centralize roll inputs when the wings are level with the hori-zon. Maintain cruise power setting.

THE SIDESLIP

The sideslip is a useful manoeuvre as it allows us to lose height rapidly without gaining too much airspeed.

To create a sideslip in a weight-shift air-craft, do not coordinate the pitch while in a turn. Therefore, as the aircraft is rolled into the turn the nose of the aircraft should be pos-itively lowered. This manoeuvre can only be maintained for a 90-degree turn.

Exercise 15

UNUSUAL AND DANGEROUS ATTITUDES/CONDITIONS

The aim of this exercise is to recognize potentially dangerous conditions of flight and to recover safely from unusual attitudes. You will see the different recoveries that are required for different unusual attitudes in the illustration below.

One thing that must be avoided with weight-shift aircraft is 'negative loading'. If at any time negative load is experienced, that is, it feels like you are floating and in some cases you can leave your seat, it is imperative that the geometry between the trike and the wing be normal. Then the only option you have is to hang on to the control bar for dear life, for transition back to normal flight.

All microlight aircraft have limitations, known as the 'envelope'. Stay within that envelope and mostly the aircraft will behave as it should, but step outside the envelope and bad things may well start to happen to the aircraft.

The limitations are:

- **VNE** Velocity never exceed.

- **VA** Manoeuvring speed, the maximum airspeed in turbulent weather.

- **Maximum bank angle** Most microlight aircraft are limited to a 60-degree bank angle.

- **Maximum pitch angle** +/– 30 degrees, some are 45 degrees.

- **Maximum 'G' loading** +4, –2, bits start to fall off beyond these loads.

Manoeuvres at these limits are unusual attitudes, but if left uncorrected may develop into dangerous conditions.

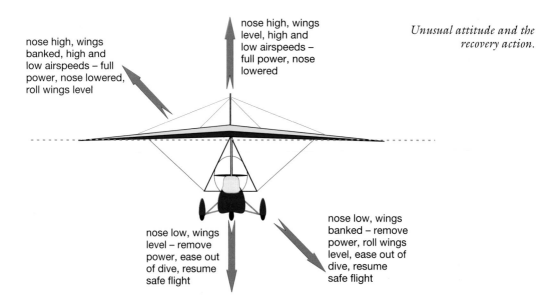

nose high, wings banked, high and low airspeeds – full power, nose lowered, roll wings level

nose high, wings level, high and low airspeeds – full power, nose lowered

Unusual attitude and the recovery action.

nose low, wings level – remove power, ease out of dive, resume safe flight

nose low, wings banked – remove power, roll wings level, ease out of dive, resume safe flight

Exercise 16a

FORCED LANDINGS WITH AND WITHOUT POWER

The aim of this exercise is to carry out a safe descent, approach and landing in the event of an engine failure during flight, and to carry out a safe unplanned precautionary landing in an unfamiliar field.

Why would an engine fail during flight? Historically, microlights have been prone to engine failures: modern 4-stroke machines are winning the war against engine failures, but even these engines can fail; with that in mind a pilot has to be able to deal with the scenario. An engine could fail because of:

- Lack of fuel
- Contaminated fuel
- Lack of lubrication
- Mechanical failure
- Pilot shutdown due to mechanical problems.

Be aware at all times during instructional flights that an instructor can spring a simulated engine failure on you at the most inconvenient times. Why? Because engines never fail when we expect them to.

Have a field choice in mind while flying around and be aware of where the wind is from: look for telltale signs such as smoke, high-standing crops, or even lakes. If the lake appears to be calm on one side and rough or rippled on the other, then the wind is coming from the calm side because the bank is sheltering the wind.

You will see from the two illustrations (*right*) that in the event of an engine failure your time in the air and the distance you could possibly travel is dictated by how high you are (based upon still air).

Based upon 500ft per minute minimum sink rate, if you adopted minimum sink from 2,000ft you could have four minutes in the air before you reach the ground, as opposed to two minutes from 1,000ft at the same descent rate.

Once you have adopted this descent rate, your choice of field and where the wind is from dictates where you will attempt to land. A mayday call might be feasible, and you could attempt a restart if time permits. Reassure your passenger if you have one.

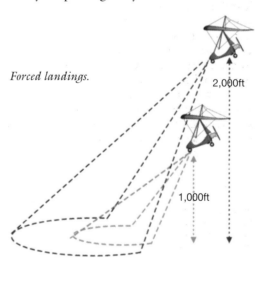

Forced landings.

2,000ft

1,000ft

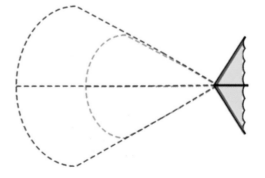

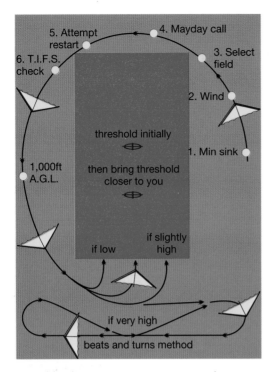

Forced landing, no power correct approaches.

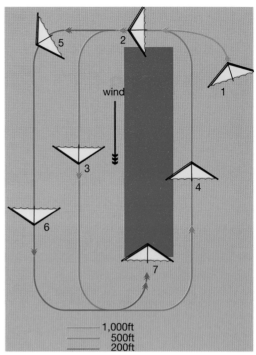

Precautionary landings.

When your engine has failed you also need to complete a series of checks to make sure that you haven't missed anything. I use a TIFS check that covers all you need for an engine failure scenario:

T Throttle off (in case the engine restarts)
I Ignition off
F Fuel tap off
S Seatbelts secure

The illustration (*above*) is a typical approach to your chosen field, and when, if time permits, you should attempt the various checks. It also shows what to do if you arrive at the field of your choice too low, too high, very high, or just right. The best way is to give yourself a constant view of your intended landing field. We call this the 'constant aspect method'; this way you can pick a spot in the middle of the field and 'home in' onto it, eventually bringing it nearer to you when on final approach. Never forget that without the engine you can always lose height but you can never get it back – it is always best to be higher rather than lower.

FORCED LANDINGS WITH POWER

The aim of this part of the exercise is to make an unplanned landing away from an airfield. Why would we make a precautionary landing?

- Passenger illness
- You are lost
- Night-time is closing in fast.
- Deteriorating weather
- Insufficient fuel

The procedure for this type of forced landing is similar to that of a complete engine failure, except that now we have power. A good check of the field you have in mind is in order, though there is still no time to relax as we have to get the aircraft on the ground quickly.

Having chosen your landing site, make a pass downwind at 1,000ft. If it looks suitable, make another pass using a circuit pattern at 500ft. If it still looks suitable, i.e. if there are no wires, fences, livestock, etc., make another pass at 200ft. This last pass will enable you to see what the surface of the landing site is like – whether it undulates unduly, how long the grass is, and so on. The illustration above will help you to picture the format.

Exercise 16b

OPERATION AT MINIMUM LEVEL

The aim of this exercise is to safely operate the aircraft at heights lower than those normally used. We might need to fly at low level because of lowering cloud perhaps, or to inspect a field in preparation for a precautionary landing. The problems we have in flying low level are the avoidance of military aircraft, Rule 5 of the Air Navigation Order (ANO), and obstacle clearance.

Low flying involving the military takes place between the heights of 250ft and 2,000ft above ground level. During this exercise, if you are flying in an AIAA (Area of Intense Aerial Activity), then a good lookout is a necessity.

Rule 5 of the ANO states that:

- A microlight aircraft shall not fly closer than 500ft to any person, vehicle, vessel or structure, except for the purpose of saving life, taking off or landing in accordance with normal aviation practice

- Also because a microlight operates on a 'Permit to Fly', it must not fly over any congested area of a city, town or settlement.

Things to be aware of while flying low level:

- Obstacles below 300ft are not marked on aeronautical charts
- Always have an active plan for an engine failure: move your track around villages, etc.
- Wind direction
- Low-level turbulence, on the lee side of hills, etc.
- Navigation is more difficult at low level because the reduced height decreases the distance it is possible to see ahead
- Monitor the engine temperatures and pressures, your airspeed and your height.

'Distance from' rule.

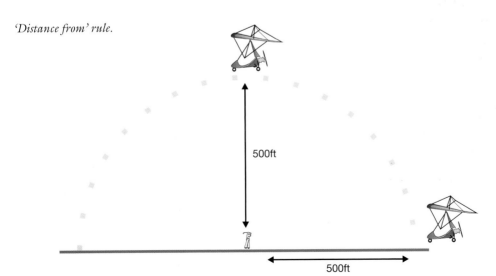

500ft

500ft

Exercises 17a, 17b and 17c

FIRST SOLO AND SOLO CONSOLIDATION

EXERCISE 17A

The aim of this exercise is to carry out a safe and accurate solo circuit, approach and landing.

As I have said before, the correct time to attempt your first solo is after all the Exercises 1–16b have been satisfactorily completed, but your instructor may have sent you solo after Exercises 12 and 13. Either way, your instructor is looking for good airmanship and the ability to handle situations that could arise with instinct. He is not looking for total perfection, he is looking for safety. With that in mind, the weather will be as near-perfect as it can get, with the wind straight down the runway, and a good, high cloud-base, if any.

Instructors sense and know when a first solo is imminent, but you have to be ready yourself, so don't be afraid to say 'no'.

Before your first solo you must have:

- A medical certificate
- An Airlaw exam pass
- Public liability insurance (check with your instructor).

Most of all, enjoy: after your first solo, the feeling of what you have accomplished never leaves you, but the moment does. Pat yourself on the back after everyone has shaken your hand, because technically you are now a pilot.

All my students do three circuits on their first solo: one at normal circuit height, without an attempt to land, to get used to the aircraft without an instructor in it; one with an approach down to 200ft followed by a go-around; then a normal circuit with, hopefully, a landing at the end of it.

EXERCISE 17B

The aim of this exercise is to practise and polish the skills learned during the dual training, and to prepare for the General Flying Test.

Usually your instructor will get in the aircraft with you to check you are still operating the aircraft and yourself in a competent manner – we call these 'check flights'. Don't be upset or surprised if permission to fly solo is refused: the weather needs to be near-perfect for your early solo work. As you gain more and more experience the weather window will expand.

You will be asked to practise differing take-off and landing techniques. You will also be asked to practise, when the circuit traffic permits, PFLs (practice forced landings) from 1,000ft overhead the airfield.

As time advances you will eventually 'break circuit' and do some local flying away from the airfield, practising the departure and rejoining methods. During these trips you may fly a triangular route that your instructor has prepared for you. Map reading, identification of local features and maintaining a compass heading are all the more important now.

You will also review the basics on your own general handling skills. I provide my students with a 'solo consolidation card' that lists various tasks to do while flying.

EXERCISE 17C

The aim of this exercise is to correct any bad habits that may have formed during your solo work, and to check that no aspect of your training has been overlooked.

This will usually take more than one session, and I like to do a 'mock' GFT to see how a student copes. There is also a ground oral aircraft technical exam, which covers rigging, de-rigging, preparation for flight, fuel and maintenance requirements, and full knowledge of the aircraft's systems and their operation.

Exercise 18

NAVIGATION

The aim of this exercise is the same for 3-axis and for weight-shift: to fly accurately and safely – in VMC and under VFR – a predetermined route, without infringing the rules governing regulated airspace. I have covered navigation in great depth on pages 40–5, so here I will cover the basics of navigation for the NPPL(M).

There is a certain amount of planning required that has to be done on the ground, then to complete the task there is a certain amount of map reading while flying. Microlights certainly aren't roomy enough to spread charts about while flying, so all the planning should be done before you even set foot to the aeroplane:

- Navigation is planning a flight from A to B
- Map reading is finding your way from A to B.

Your first ports of call, as it were, in planning a flight are:

- To check NOTAMS, which tell you if any unusual aerial activity will affect your chosen route such as Royal flights, RAF manoeuvres, flying displays, etc.
- To check the weather, by means of TAF and METAR, and by flight briefing charts and spot wind charts, which are readily available from the Met Office by fax or the web
- Make sure your chart is current and correct for the area you are flying in
- My personal preference is to call the destination airfield to PPR (Prior Permission Required). This enables two things: 1) for you to find out any information that may be applicable about the destination; and 2) the destination airfield

knows you are coming and can brief you on any changes that may have occurred since publication of their entries in guides such as *Pooleys*.

If all is well, then and only then plan your route. The main things to remember while planning a route are:

- Landing sites: if something should go wrong you need to stay within the law, so plan your route so that you avoid towns and villages, etc.
- If your journey is a long one, plan your fuel, there is a serious lack of petrol stations at 2,000ft and you need to have enough to get to a refuelling point, while giving yourself a good 30 minutes' reserve
- If you are in a 3-axis machine, make sure that it is correctly loaded and not overloaded, either with people or by luggage. There are calculations that can be made to make sure that you remain within the 'envelope'. Weight-shift aircraft are a little different, but even these aircraft types have MTOW (Maximum Take-Off Weight) that must not be exceeded
- If you are using airband radio while flying, then the QNH is readily obtainable for the ASR (Altimeter Setting Region) you are flying in, as will be the QFE at your destination airfield
- If you are non-radio, then to find out the QNH set your altimeter while at your home airfield to zero, then add the height of your airfield. For example, if the altimeter reads zero at 1000Mb, add the height of your airfield – say 90ft – and in this case you will get a QNH setting of

997Mb (remember that air pressure decreases by 1Mb every 30ft).

Depart from your airfield's overhead, or you will be setting a heading on the compass parallel to your track, which is all well and good but not correct. Better still, depart from a known point such as a local landmark away from your home airfield.

While flying your route, trust your compass – has it lied to you before? I doubt it, so why not trust it now. Because microlight aircraft travel at slow to medium airspeeds, maintenance of a heading only needs to be within +/–10 degrees. Remember also that your timings are from overhead to overhead, not from take off to landing.

During the planning phase of your flight have an alternate airfield in mind and plan a route from your chosen destination airfield to the alternate. This is in case something has happened at your original airfield.

Be aware of sudden changes in weather that could prohibit you completing your task and never be afraid to return home. It's better to be safe on the ground at home, and fly another day. Keep checking behind, to check the weather also, remembering you have to get back. What is the point in continuing if you can't return?

If for any reason you get lost while flying your planned route, and you knew where you were 15 minutes ago, either return to that point and try again, or return home. If neither of these options are available, don't be afraid to carry out a precautionary landing to find out your position. If all else fails and you are using an airband radio, call up on the emergency frequency (121.50): they will help, so never be afraid to use this facility.

On arrival at your destination airfield, forewarned is forearmed, so call the airfield on the radio and check QFE, runway in use, etc. Fly the correct circuit and land, and follow instructions on the ground if asked to do so. Park and leave the aircraft in a secure and safe position, and make your way to the booking in office and pay any landing fees due.

You will during your course of training be required to complete two dual cross-country flights, to differing airfields, and two solo cross-country flights, though the dual portion of this exercise is not mandatory. Your solo flights must be to a different airfield more than 15nm away and be a minimum 40nm round trip.

Common Problems that Students Face During Exercises

Exercises 1–3
During Exercises 1–3 there aren't many problems experienced by a student, perhaps a little apprehension if the student hasn't flown before.

Exercise 4
- Under/over banking
- Handling the controls incorrectly
- Pitch oscillating
- In some cases making reverse control inputs, although this is more probable with 3-axis students converting to weight-shift.

Exercise 5
- Reverse nosewheel inputs – again more common with 3-axis students
- Misuse of the throttle
- Taxiing too slow or too fast
- Not taking account of the wind direction, especially in weight-shift aircraft
- Not anticipating a turn while taxiing.

Exercise 6
- Most students have a bad airmanship day during this lesson
- Gripping the base bar or the control column too tight
- Incorrect power settings for level flight
- Instruments holding a fascination for the student
- Over/under controlling.

Exercise 7
- Airmanship
- Getting the mnemonic PA(H)T wrong and raising the nose before applying power

- Not climbing straight
- Failing to check the temperatures and pressures during a climb
- When levelling out, getting APT wrong by reducing power before adjusting attitude.

Exercise 8
- Airmanship can still be a problem
- PA(H)T can be wrong again, reducing the power before lowering the nose
- Not warming the engine on long glide descents
- Not anticipating the levelling-off height
- Over-descending.

Exercise 9
- Bad airmanship yet again
- Failing to look before a turn
- Insufficient entry airspeed
- A tendency to over-bank
- Failure to anticipate and roll out on a heading
- Incorrect pitch and bank attitudes
- In 3-axis types, failure to maintain balance.

Exercise 10
- Failure to complete a HASELL check correctly
- Not maintaining shallow angles of bank during slow flight
- Not maintaining correct attitude and airspeed during slow flight
- Not keeping wings level during a full stall
- Not entering a fully developed stall
- Lack of coordination with power, usually

not applying enough during standard stall recovery.

Exercise 11
Although this exercise is not flown, during a wing-drop stall the student may try to pick up the lower wing with aileron.

Exercise 12 and 13
- Not maintaining the centreline of the runway
- Not having the incorrect power setting for take-off
- Not allowing for drift during the circuit
- Not levelling out at circuit height
- Not making pre-landing checks
- Approaching either too fast or too slow
- Relaxing after touchdown.

Exercise 14
- Failure to complete a HASELL check
- Insufficient power and pitch coordination and so not maintaining level flight during the turn
- Not looking into the turn
- Not anticipating the roll-out point
- An incorrect sequence for recovery from a spiral dive.

Exercise 15
- HASELL check missed again or incomplete
- Totally wrong assessment of the condition
- Incorrect recovery procedure for minimum height loss.

Exercise 16
- Failure to correctly choose a suitable landing site
- Incorrect assessment of the wind direction
- Failure to trim for best glide speed
- Not attempting a re-start when time is available
- Failure to increase airspeed in the final stages of approach
- Incorrect procedure and height assessment for a precautionary landing
- Failure to complete a TIFS check.

Exercise 17
- Adopting bad habits
- Getting complacent
- Ground checks poorly executed.

Exercise 18
- Poor route planning
- Failure to advise anyone of non-arrival or late arrival
- Failure to PPR
- Incorrectly joining the circuit at the destination airfield.

Sample Questions

1. In steady level flight, what are the four forces?

a) Lift, weight, drag, thrust.
b) Lift, load, drag, thrust.
c) Lift, load, drag, power.

2. When an aircraft is at a constant speed and altitude what is this known as?

a) Balanced.
b) Equilibrium.
c) In a straight line.

3. At what angle is lift in relation to the airflow?

a) 90°.
b) 80°.
c) It depends if you are climbing or descending.

4. When the aircraft stalls, what is actually happening?

a) The airflow is no longer laminar over the top of the aerofoil.
b) The wind has stopped blowing.
c) The engine has stopped.

5. Why must we complete a series of checks before we fly any aircraft?

a) Because the instructor says so.
b) Because it's your last chance to find any faults before you fly.
c) Because the Wright brothers did them.

6. What is the difference between QFE and QNH?

a) Nothing.
b) Airfield elevation and sea level.
c) Sea level and flight above 3,000ft.

7. To remain VFR, what must we be in sight of at all times?

a) The airfield.
b) The ground.
c) Your instructor.

8. What is the DALR?

a) When you are thirsty and need a drink.
b) 3°C loss of temperature for every 1,000ft you ascend.
c) 1.5°C loss of temperature for every 1,000ft you ascend.

9. A thunderstorm needs certain criteria; these are?

a) Hot and humid air, unstable conditions and a lifting force.
b) Hot and humid air, stable conditions, and a lifting force.
c) Sun, clear skies and warm temperatures.

10. What is precipitation?

a) Rain, snow, sleet, hail, drizzle.
b) Taking part.
c) Unstable air.

11. Flying above an airfield, you see a white cross on a runway; what does this mean?

a) Bet you can't land there.
b) Unsuitable for landing and manoeuvring.
c) The controller is angry.

12. Compared to a tarmac runway, grass that is wet will ... take-off run?

a) Increase the.
b) Decrease the.
c) Have the same.

13. How does the airspeed indicator work?

a) It measures dynamic pressure.
b) It measures how fast the wheels are turning.
c) It measures how fast the propeller is turning.

14. In its simplest form, what is an altimeter?

a) A barometer.
b) A vertical measuring device.
c) An all-time measuring device.

15. When approaching an airfield with the intention of landing, do you trust what the ... as to which runway to use?

a) Radio operator has told you.
b) Signal square tells you.
c) Windsock tells you.

16. You have landed in a field after an engine failure. Who do you inform, assuming you and your passenger are uninjured and the aircraft is in one piece?

a) Your wife, because you're going to be late.
b) The landowner.
c) Nobody.

17. In microlights there is a rule that states we must not fly ... 500ft?

a) Lower than.
b) Nearer than.
c) Over.

18. What is a pitot tube for?

a) Siphoning petrol.
b) Directing dynamic pressure towards the altimeter.
c) Venting the fuel tank.

19. Most aerodromes have number on their runways; what do these numbers mean?

a) The amount of pounds it costs to land.
b) The magnetic direction of the runway.
c) The true direction of the runway.

20. A microlight aircraft requires what minimum instrumentation?

a) Compass, altimeter, airspeed indicator.
b) Compass, altimeter, tachometer (RPM gauge).
c) Altimeter, compass, EGT gauges.

21. A restricted microlight licence restricts you from flying when what?

a) The cloud base is below 1,000ft and the wind is above 15kt.
b) All the above and going farther than 8nm from your take-off point.
c) You are full of fuel.

22. While flying a microlight, do you need a chart to be legal?

a) Yes.
b) Yes, and it must be current and for the area you are flying in.
c) No, a GPS will suffice.

ANSWERS

1) a.
2) b.
3) a.
4) a.
5) b.
6) b.
7) b.
8) b.
9) a.
10) a.
11) b.
12) a.

13) a.
14) a.
15) c.
16) b.
17) b.
18) b.
19) b.
20) a.
21) b.
22) b.

The questions in the previous pages are designed on the same format as the microlight exams, multiple choice.

Index